D1282186

AMERICA AND THE PROGRESSIVE ERA 1900–1917

AMERICA AND THE PROGRESSIVE ERA 1900–1917

FON W. BOARDMAN, JR.

New York
HENRY Z. WALCK, INC.

To the memory of my brother
Robert E. Boardman

Copyright © 1970 by Fon W. Boardman, Jr.
All rights reserved
ISBN: 0–8098–3084–1
Library of Congress Catalog Card Number: 70–87244
Printed in the United States of America

This Main Entry catalog card may be reproduced without permission.

973.9 Boardman, Fon W.
B America and the progressive era: 1900-1917, by Fon W. Boardman, Jr. Walck, 1970
169p.

Reading list: p. 161-164. Index.
Political, economic, and social survey of America from the turn of the century to the start of World War I.

1. U.S. - History - 1898-1919
2. U.S. - Social life and customs
I. Title

J
973.9
B63
(12-)

Contents

N. METH. 7-29-70 $4.71

100963

AMERICA AND THE PROGRESSIVE ERA 1900–1917

1 *America and the New Century*

THE WORLD's newest imperial power, the United States of America, greeted January 1, 1900, the beginning of the twentieth century, with confidence. It was a prosperous, growing nation whose flag flew over territory extending from islands in the Atlantic Ocean westward to the far side of the Pacific Ocean.

The Civil War had ended nearly thirty-five years before and a whole new generation had been born since the surrender at Appomattox. The veterans of that war, who had been young men in 1865, were now the middle-aged leaders of business and politics. Their organization, the Grand Army of the Republic, was influential at the highest levels, and in the North thousands of persons still voted for the Republican Party because "they saved the Union, didn't they?" Even so, North and South had been reconciled and events of the post-war years had brought the nation together again.

The country was still very rural and old-fashioned in spirit, even though there were many signs of change. Independence Day was celebrated with fireworks and parades in every small town. Ice-cream parlors did a good business after the band concert in the village square. Most town houses were still lighted by gas, and refrigeration was achieved with the aid of the iceman and the large cakes of ice he brought. Horses were everywhere, pulling all kinds of carriages and wagons, but already there were nearly 14,000 automobiles and the number was growing. Wages were low by later standards, but so were prices. Sofas were advertised at $9.98, turtleneck sweaters were eight cents each, and a man could buy a good quality suit for under $11.00.

The population of the United States reached 76,000,000 in 1900, double what it had been in 1870. By 1910 there would be more than 90,000,000 Americans; by the time the country entered World War I in 1917, the population would pass the 100,000,000 mark. An important part of the nineteenth-century growth in population resulted from immigration: from 1870 to 1900 nearly 12,000,000 persons came to America's shores, mostly from Europe. Such newcomers were continuing to arrive at an average rate of about 1,000,000 a year.

At the same time, a much larger proportion of the American people—native and immigrant alike—was living in urban rather than rural areas. In 1870 there were only seven cities in the whole broad country that could boast of 200,000 or more inhabitants; in thirty years this number grew to nineteen.

Changes in the economic life of the country were as great and even more significant than population growth. The last decade or so of the old century marked the end of one era and the beginning of another. The frontier, which had moved steadily westward for generations, disappeared about 1890. Industry, for the first time, became more important than agriculture, and also became more dependent on machinery than on skilled labor. It was organized in ever larger units while the "trusts" and the holding companies began to dominate one field of enterprise after another. By 1900 there were 185 large industrial combinations whose total capitalization of $3,000,000,000 represented one-third of all the capital in all the nation's manufacturing enterprises.

The middle years of the 1890's had been a period of business depression, but conditions began to improve in 1897 and most Americans were optimistic as the new century dawned. This was true in spite of the fact that class and economic distinctions were steadily—

and some thought dangerously—increasing. Almost all the wealth of the country was controlled by about 20 per cent of the people. Working men, who labored in units of hundreds and thousands, no longer had any direct contact with those who owned or controlled the enormous factories. Then, too, more and more of the actual control was exercised by bankers and financiers rather than by industrialists and factory managers. The farmers of the West and South felt themselves going down in both economic and social status. They loudly blamed the bankers and the railroad owners for their troubles, claiming that they could borrow money only at exorbitant rates of interest, and that the railroads were charging them far too much to transport their products.

Certainly the country was entering a period of increased tension among its member groups, in both economics and politics. The new century might look enticing, but it brought with it terrifying problems in adjusting to the new urban industrialized world. There was the need to absorb the masses of immigrants, most of whom lived in poverty in the large cities; to bridge the gap between the new gaudy rich and the landless factory hands; to bring up to date the antiquated political machinery so that a continent and its large cities could be governed honestly and efficiently.

No event of the last years of the old century did more to change the world for Americans than the Spanish-American War in 1898. What started out for many well-meaning people as a struggle to free Cuba and the Cubans from oppressive Spanish rule ended as a war of conquest that presented the United States with a colonial empire. In ten weeks in the spring and summer, American naval and military strength toppled Spain as a world power, and made for this country a place in the ranks of imperial glory. The peace treaty that followed confirmed the American democracy as ruler of Puerto Rico in the Atlantic, and of the Philippine Islands in the Pacific, with their native and Spanish cultures and languages. In a separate and peaceful transaction the Hawaiian Islands were annexed in 1898 and became a territory in 1900. By agreement with Germany and Great Britain, seven islands in the Samoan group in the Pacific became United States property in 1899.

The Puerto Ricans preferred American to Spanish rule, but many Filipinos felt otherwise. Those who had been fighting the Spanish regime expected the United States to give the islands their freedom, as it was doing in Cuba, and they declared their independence in early 1899. The men in authority in Washington did not think the Filipinos were as yet capable of self-government, and saw the native government as an insurrection. Before the bloody struggle that followed was ended, American forces in the islands amounted to 74,000 men, and there were unpleasant charges of atrocities on both sides. In 1900 William Howard Taft was sent to the Philippines to establish a civil government, but it was 1902 before the war could be officially ended and a basic law for the islands passed by Congress.

Taft's good sense and genial nature while he was governor of the islands from 1901 to 1904 did much to reconcile the Filipinos to American rule. He placed primary emphasis on education, and he resolved diplomatically a dispute over lands owned by the Roman Catholic Church. In 1916 a new law gave the citizens of the island full legislative power, but executive authority continued to be held by an American governor general.

The nation's leader at the opening of the twentieth century was William McKinley, born in Niles, Ohio, in 1843. He was a veteran of the Union Army in the Civil War, from which he had returned a major. After serving in Congress and as governor of Ohio, with the Cleveland industrialist and chairman of the Republican National Committee Mark Hanna as his chief supporter, he easily won the Republican nomination for the presidency in 1896. In one of the noisiest and bitterest campaigns ever staged, he defeated young William Jennings Bryan (1860–1925), the Democratic candidate. The campaign was fought on the issue of maintaining the gold standard, which the Republicans favored, versus permitting the unlimited coinage of silver and its acceptance as a monetary standard along with gold. McKinley received 271 electoral votes to 176 for Bryan.

Once in office, McKinley had to turn his attention chiefly to foreign affairs. He made sincere efforts to settle the Cuban rebellion without American intervention, but the pressures on him became too great. He eventually advocated armed intervention against Spain, and when the war ended in complete American victory he decided, after some soul-searching, that the Philippines should be annexed. In 1900 he was renominated and defeated Bryan by a greater margin than before—292 to 155 electoral votes. In this election Bryan chose to make anti-imperialism his main issue. Although he sternly denounced the acquisition of the former Spanish colonies, the majority of the people did not agree. The Republicans stuck to their theme that the nation was prosperous because of Republican rule. With business booming and with farmers doing somewhat better than usual, the party in power had little trouble in staying there.

Early in his second term, in September, 1901, President McKinley went to Buffalo, New York, to make a speech at the Pan-American Exposition. There, on September 6, he was shot twice by a young anarchist, Leon Czolgosz, who stood in the receiving line at a reception with a pistol concealed in a handkerchief. When he reached the President, he pulled the trigger, firing point-blank into his abdomen. For a few days McKinley seemed to be recovering, but he took a turn for the worse and died on September 14. The assassin was tried, convicted and electrocuted before the end of October.

The career of the last veteran of the Civil War to be president ended with an assassin's bullet. A handsome, kindly, genial man, McKinley was anxious to do the right thing and what was best for the country; and he firmly believed that this goal could be achieved by following established Republican policies. If the nation stayed on the gold standard, if tariff rates were kept high, and if the businessmen and financiers were allowed to operate the economic machinery as they thought best, the nation would prosper.

McKinley's successor was Vice-President Theodore Roosevelt, not quite forty-three years old and the youngest man ever to become president of the United States. He represented a new generation and his name and his actions—along with those of Woodrow Wilson—became synonymous with the period in the nation's history that ended with World War I. Roosevelt was born in New York City on October 27, 1858, to a well-placed, well-to-do family. His childhood was easy and pleasant except that he was not a strong boy. His eyes were weak and he had asthma. He was determined to overcome his physical frailty and in the course of the years he succeeded in living a strenuous athletic life.

While still at Harvard he began writing his first book, which was published in 1882—a sound, favorably reviewed book, *The Naval War of 1812*. In the meantime, in 1881, he entered politics, which not many young men of his social class did at that time. He won election as a Republican to the New York State Assembly and served from 1881 to 1884. At first he caused some amusement with his "dude" clothing and his high-pitched voice, but his energy and determination made him an effective legislator. The constant activity, the voice, and, most of all, the enormous grin that seemed to reveal innumerable teeth became his trademark and a priceless gift to the newspaper cartoonists.

Depressed by the death of his first wife, in 1884 Roosevelt went to the badlands of Dakota Territory, where he had bought a ranch. Here he spent two years, at first laughed at as he had been in the Assembly for his Eastern ways, but he won the respect of the cowboys by the way he entered into their strenuous life. His interest in the West eventually resulted in four volumes worthy of a professional historian, *The Winning of the West* (1889–96). Returning to New York, he plunged back into politics, running for the office of mayor of the city in 1886, but ending up a rather poor third. President Benjamin Harrison appointed him to the United States Civil Service Commission in 1889 and a Democratic president, Grover Cleveland, had him continue in that post.

In 1895 Roosevelt was appointed a commissioner of the Police Board of New York City and was elected its president. In effect, this made him police commissioner. He took to prowling the streets late at night, wearing a dark cloak and a hat pulled down over his face in an attempt to hide his famous teeth, while he sought policemen who might be neglecting their duty. Two years later the new president, William McKinley, somewhat reluctantly appointed Roosevelt assistant-secretary of the Navy. It was a post he greatly desired, but already his saber-rattling remarks in favor of American expansion had the peaceable McKinley worried.

Those worries were well-founded. In February, 1898, when the Secretary of the Navy was absent from his office, Roosevelt took it upon himself to send instructions to Commodore George Dewey to make sure his Asiatic Squadron was ready to fight the Spanish Navy in the Pacific Ocean the moment war was declared. The eventual result of this action was the naval victory in Manila Bay on May 1. When war came, a desk job in Washington was too tame for Roosevelt. He received permission, along with Colonel Leonard Wood under whom he was supposed to serve, to form a volunteer cavalry regiment. Although it had a formal designation, the unit was soon known as the Rough Riders, and Roosevelt was its leading spirit. The regiment was made up of an undisciplined mixture of cowboys and Indians from the West and Ivy Leaguish young men from the East. The Rough Riders had to leave their horses behind, but they were soon in the thick of things in Cuba. On July 1, 1898, Roosevelt got his chance to lead his men in a charge up San Juan Hill. Roosevelt performed bravely and became a national hero.

The Republican leaders of New York State decided that a war hero was just what they needed, and they made Colonel Roosevelt their candidate for the governorship that same year. Roosevelt won, but by fewer than 18,000 votes. He was such an ambitious governor, especially in his zeal to root out corruption, that in 1900 some Republican leaders were only too happy to have him nominated for the vice-presidency, in which it was normal for a man to disappear from public view.

Now, not much more than a year later, the Harvard educated, rough-riding cowboy with the squeaky voice was president of the United States. The public soon showed genuine fondness for their first exciting presidential personality in many years. He had married again and had five more children, all of whom were encouraged to make the sedate White House a place for fun. He began work early, he worked hard, he played hard. At one time he became an advocate of simplified spelling, but his enthusiasm soon wore off.

Roosevelt was well prepared by his background, his education and his interests to deal with the new problems facing the recently industrialized and imperialistic nation. By nature, he saw all public issues, whether domestic or foreign, in moral terms. At the same time, he owed his political success to the Republican Party which was dominated by big business interests. Thus, while he was at heart in sympathy with the reform mood of large numbers of people, he was not ready to push for drastic changes; nor was he in a position to do so as chief of a Republican administration with a majority in both houses of the Congress. His first message to that Congress, in December, 1901, seemed conservative enough. However, he did say flatly that the existing laws and attitudes concerning great wealth and monopolistic business were "no longer sufficient." He was trying to express his beliefs and objectives, while still recognizing that he could not get a conservative Congress to go very far along his chosen path all at once.

Domestically, Roosevelt's biggest problem was that posed by the growing concentration of industrial and financial power: to what extent, if any, should the Federal government control or regulate—or dissolve—this new type of business organization popularly known as a "trust?" In foreign affairs Roosevelt was happy to play the role of chief of a mighty nation concerned with peace and war in Europe and Asia.

A particular field of possible achievement that interested him was that of the conservation of natural resources. Although a small start had been made a dozen years before, by setting aside some Federally owned land as forest reserves and parks, it was Theodore Roosevelt who first brought conservation to the nation's attention and who put a comprehensive policy into effect. Roosevelt's interest stemmed from his love of the outdoors and from his experiences in the West. With his strong support, the Newlands Act became law in 1902. This law authorized the government to build irrigation projects in sixteen Western states, and to use the proceeds from the sale of such irrigated land for further projects. A forest conservation program was consolidated and pushed by the dedicated Gifford Pinchot, the first American professional forester. When Roosevelt took office there were about 45,000,000 acres of land in the government reserves. During his time as president he added almost 150,000,000 acres. At one point, faced with a bill from Congress that would require that body's approval before any more forest reserves were created in certain states, Roosevelt gleefully established or increased thirty-two such reserves just before signing the bill into law.

At Roosevelt's urging, a Department of Commerce and Labor was established by law in 1903, and it included a Bureau of Corporations with authority to investigate the conduct of corporations engaged in interstate business. This was the first step in the president's program for dealing with the new business giants.

By 1904, when it was time for another presidential election, Roosevelt had achieved wide popularity with the people and had consolidated his power within the Republican Party. He was easily nominated and was opposed, in a dull campaign, by Judge Alton B. Parker, a conservative Democrat. The energetic incumbent was elected by an unprecedented margin of popular votes—something over 2,500,000—and received 336 electoral votes to Parker's 140. He was now president in his own right. He was also the most prominent leader of the progressive movement, whose program and activities determined the tone and temper of American politics until domestic reform, partly achieved, was eclipsed by the turmoil of World War I.

Theodore Roosevelt and the progressive movement had much in common. Both the President and the leaders of the progressives thrived on idealism and moral struggle, while in both cases the goals sought were clearer to them than the practical methods necessary to achieve those goals. Some aspects of the movement were inherited from the Populist agitation of the latter years of the nineteenth century. This was chiefly a southern and midwestern agrarian revolt against industry and finance. It was also, in its unspoken ideals, a nostalgic desire to turn back the clock, to keep America simple and rural. The progressives, while they sought the support of this same agricultural America, were urban-oriented and were concerned primarily with the problems of industrial monopolies, corruption in government, assimilation of the new immigrants, and the relief of the poverty that accompanied the new industrial order.

Unfortunately, they were not as forward-looking as they believed they were. They were honest beyond doubt, they were disinterested and sought nothing for themselves—except, perhaps, that some of them thought they deserved to rule over their less-favored neighbors. They did not believe the new industrial revolution could be denied, but they hoped to solve the problem of too much power in the hands of the great corporations by breaking those giants up into smaller units.

While in some measure they sought a better lot for the worker, at heart they feared labor unions almost as much as they did corporations, and for the same reasons: they too might become powerful and monopolistic. They wanted also to "Americanize" the immigrants so they would be better citizens, but in truth they looked down on the foreign-speaking, badly dressed, uneducated men and women who were arriving in large numbers every year from Europe. They did believe in democracy and they did believe that human nature could be changed by education. They believed in progress, but it was a progress that had as its goal a world in which all would emulate their manners and morals as well as behave like good citizens in political affairs. Most of the progressives were urban, middle-class Protestants, professional men or with inherited money, and college educated. There were progressives in both the Republican and the Democratic Party. At first, they worked mainly through the Republicans and Theodore Roosevelt; later Woodrow Wilson and the Democrats served the cause better. Whatever the process, the progressives did succeed in securing a good deal of legislation that embodied their ideals. This legislation was intended to regulate railroads and business; to make the democratic process more responsive to the individual voter, by such methods as the direct recall of office-holders by popular vote; and to run cities on a businesslike basis. The progressives fought for the imposition of corporation and personal income taxes, the direct election of senators, and a government-controlled central banking system.

As president, Roosevelt was looked to for leadership in the fight for progressive goals, but he sometimes disappointed his followers. He did get more radical as time went on. Toward the end of his second term he proposed that the stock market be regulated; argued that the laboring man should get "a larger share of the wealth" he produced; and denounced "the speculative folly and the flagrant dishonesty of a few men of great wealth." A start was made, and some specific steps taken, but Roosevelt's chief contribution to the cause is generally conceded to be the publicity he gave it.

Some of the most effective work of the progressives was done at the state and municipal level. Robert M. LaFollette (1885–1925), who was later the progressive leader in the United States Senate, showed as governor of Wisconsin from 1900 to 1904 what could be done to rid a state of domination by selfish groups—in this case the railroad and lumber industries—and to govern in the interests of the people in general. This kind of reform administration won control in other states, especially in the West.

At the city level, there were reform mayors such as Samuel (Golden Rule) Jones and Brand Whitlock of Toledo, Ohio, and Tom L. Johnson of Cleveland, Ohio. Jones, a successful businessman, was first elected in 1897. The reforms he instituted, which included an eight-hour day and a minimum wage for city employees, angered the Republican politicians so that they refused to renominate him. He ran three times thereafter as an independent, and died in office. He was succeeded by Whitlock, who wrote two novels about municipal politics while in office, and later became ambassador to Belgium during World War I. Johnson, who earned a fortune with his streetcar and steel interests, served four terms as mayor of Cleveland. Although he did not succeed in putting through municipal ownership of utilities—another favorite goal of the progressives—he did make Cleveland the best-governed city in the nation.

Journalism and publicity played important roles in promoting the goals of the progressives, especially with regard to corruption in government and the monopolistic practices of business and industry. During the period, scores of articles appeared in magazines—revealing the truth, as the reformers saw it—about the way America was really ruled. Novels were also written to expose evil. The use of journalism to further a social cause was made possible by new magazines of mass circulation, a number of them counting their readers in the hundreds of thousands. Such magazines included *McClure's, Munsey's, Everybody's, Cosmopolitan, Collier's,* and the *American Magazine.* The men and women who wrote these articles were called muckrakers, although the name was applied some time after they began their work. It was applied to them in 1906 by Theodore Roosevelt who, while basically on their side, feared their revelations would get people too worked up and indignant.

Lincoln Steffens was the best-known of the muckrakers, his first article on corruption in city government appearing in 1902. As he went around the country studying such cities as St. Louis, Chicago and New York, he came to the conclusion that the presumably honest businessman was most to blame for corrupt city government. It was he who offered the bribes and made the deals with the politicians that gained him lucrative franchises for street railways and public utilities at little cost. Steffens's articles of this kind were collected as *The Shame of the Cities.* Shortly after Steffens began writing, Ida M. Tarbell's *History of the Standard Oil Company,* with an account of the practices that enabled John D. Rockefeller and his colleagues to dominate the new petroleum industry, became the outstanding exposé of the evils of business. Ray Stannard Baker's *Railroads on Trial* and Burton J. Hendrick's *Story of Life Insurance* created public demand for reform and regulation. David Graham Phillips' *The Treason of the Senate* carried the attack to the highest legislative level, but unlike most of the other muckrakers, he was not as careful with his facts as he should have been.

But while the progressive movement, with the aid of some political leaders, was opening this twentieth-century battle for reform, American industry and finance were daily growing in wealth and power in the new economic world.

2 *The Age of the Trusts*

THE ECONOMIC WORLD in which Americans lived had been changing rapidly ever since the end of the Civil War, and as the years passed it seemed to change even faster. In 1894 the United States took first place among all nations in the value of its manufactured products. By 1900 the value of these products was twice that of all agricultural goods produced on the nation's farms.

A more subtle change was in the way business was organized, managed and controlled. The day of the small firm—with limited capital and owned by one man, or by a few partners—was over as far as the important industries were concerned. The corporate form of organization was now preferred. For one thing, large amounts of capital were required and could be secured only by selling quantities of stocks and bonds. This gave a voice in management—sometimes the dominant voice—to the bankers and financiers. The day of the owner-manager was giving way to a more collective system in which experts in different fields attempted to apply scientific methods to management as well as to mechanical processes. Finally, individual companies and factories not only grew larger but also began to merge. Around the turn of the century there was an actual decline in the number of separate companies in some industries. In the largest and most profitable fields, mergers were creating a single organization, or at most two or three, which could control production, wages and prices in an entire industry. The wishes or the welfare of employees and customers could be ignored. In just three years, from 1899 to 1902, seventy-nine of these large-scale mergers were completed, involving firms with a combined capital of more than $4,000,000,000.

While the progressives were agitating for the control and regulation of these swollen businesses that seemed to them irresponsible monstrosities, most of the men who were busy creating the new industrial order, and profiting greatly from it, saw the process as the working out of natural law. During the 1902 coal strike, George F. Baer, a railroad president, declared that the laboring man would be taken care of "by the Christian men to whom God, in his infinite wisdom, has given control of the property interests of the country."

Just what was a "trust" about which there was now so much controversy? This organizational scheme was first used in the early 1880's. Each of the individuals or groups that controlled a particular business firm deposited its stock with a board of trustees and was given trust certificates in return. The trustee group could then use the stocks left with it to control and coordinate the operations of all the firms involved. This eliminated competition and often left the public at the mercy of the trust. When laws and courts began to frown on this form of control, the corporation lawyers turned to the holding company arrangement, which was legal in some states. In this process a new company was formed, which then bought a controlling interest in the stock of the other companies involved. Usually no cash was required, as the holding company simply issued stocks and bonds which it exchanged for the securities of the individual firms. The holding company was the legal form used most widely in the early years of the twentieth century.

Whatever the form, the word "trust" took hold of the imagination of cartoonists, editorial writers and reformers, and became a term denoting something evil and rapacious. Another muckraker, John Moody, writing in *The Truth about the Trusts* in 1904, put their number at 318 at that time. Some of the best known—or most notorious—were the Sugar Trust, the Whiskey Trust, the Tobacco Trust and the Rubber Trust. There was even an international Sewing Thread Trust which came into being in 1901 when British and American firms joined forces.

The largest combination of the era, and the nation's first billion-dollar business, was the United States Steel Corporation, formed in early 1901 after some months of negotiation. The banker who masterminded the deal that combined nearly a dozen steel companies into one gigantic holding company was J. P. Morgan. The new company issued stocks and bonds totalling a little more than $1,400,000,000 to pay for the concerns it was taking over. At the time, about half of this represented no real assets, in that it exceeded the previous valuation placed on the various companies by that amount. This half represented hopes for the future, profits for those who sold their firms, and commissions for the banking syndicate that handled the stock issue. Morgan and the others in this last group ended up with $62,500,000 profit.

United States Steel not only produced iron and steel products, but also owned coal mines and iron ore, cargo ships and railroads. It employed 168,000 men, and its plants, machinery and management, protected by a high tariff on imports, combined to form one of the most productive and efficient industrial complexes in the world. If any one man was responsible for the growth of the American steel industry, it was Andrew Carnegie, who also profited the most—receiving $250,000,000 as his share for the Carnegie Steel Company when it became the largest single unit of the new mammoth holding company.

Carnegie was born in Scotland in 1825, the son of a weaver who emigrated to Pennsylvania. The young Carnegie worked first in a cotton mill, then for the Pennsylvania Railroad. He saved his earnings so diligently and invested them so wisely in oil and railroads that by the time he was thirty he was able to devote himself entirely to his interests in iron manufacturing. By 1900 the Carnegie Steel Company was producing a quarter of all the steel made in the United States. After Carnegie sold out, the income from his share of this deal alone was $12,500,000 a year, at a time when there was no income tax. Some of the money went into a 32,000-acre estate in his native Scotland.

The first attempt to deal with the growing power of industrial and railroad combinations was made in 1890 when the Sherman Antitrust Act became law. This law stated that "Every contract, combination in the form of trust or otherwise, or conspiracy, in restraint of trade or commerce among the several States, or with foreign nations, is hereby declared to be illegal." It was, however, vague and general enough in its wording so that the conservative courts could interpret it in such a way that the trusts were scarcely hindered. In 1914 President Woodrow Wilson asked for legislation that would clarify and strengthen the Sherman Act. The result was the Clayton Antitrust Act which was more specific in forbidding practices which "substantially tended" to lessen competition, such as price-fixing. Again, the conservative courts largely nullified the intentions of those who sought to control trusts and monopolies by this kind of legislation. Another part of President Wilson's antitrust program was the establishment, also in 1914, of the Federal Trade Commission. It was intended to end unfair competition, to prevent the publication of false and deceptive advertising, and, in general, to investigate alleged violations of antitrust laws.

The three presidents of the period, including two Republicans (Roosevelt and Taft) and one Democrat (Wilson), were more concerned with the regulation of trusts than with any other domestic issue. Roosevelt was the first president to challenge big business and to insist that the public and labor also had some rights. Under his administration a good many antitrust lawsuits were started, and no one was more vigorous in publicly condemning the evils of monopoly. Yet Roosevelt never wanted to destroy large industrial organizations. He realized their inevitability in the new technological world and saw the benefits that could come from them. He did want the Federal government to control the trusts in the general interest of the country, and to punish those which did wrong.

By nature Taft was more conservative than Roosevelt, and also less given to flamboyant public expressions of his opinions. Nevertheless, he too carried on an active fight against the trusts and began even more suits in the courts. He wanted to require Federal rather than state incorporation of businesses engaged in interstate commerce. He asked for, but did not get, legislation which would set up a body somewhat similar to the Federal Trade Commission that was established a few years later. Taft believed firmly in the capitalistic system and thought that the antitrust laws could be used to enforce competition effectively. Wilson believed that if there were definite rules defining unfair practices most businessmen would be glad to abide by them. He saw a difference between big business that was honestly competitive, and trusts whose chief purpose was to eliminate competition. Gradually he put less reliance on trying to define every unfair practice in legislative acts and more on regulation by a commission. However, the Federal Trade Commission was somewhat of a disappointment. Wilson did not appoint men as zealous in keeping a suspicious eye on big business as the sponsors of the legislation had anticipated.

Many trusts and large businesses figured in antitrust lawsuits, including the American Sugar Refining Company, the United States Steel Corporation and the American Tobacco Company. Two of the most significant cases were those involving the Standard Oil Company and the Northern Securities Company.

Only a generation earlier the petroleum industry had been new, but it grew rapidly in size and importance as the internal combustion engine became more widely used. In 1900, 63 million barrels of crude oil were pumped out of the ground. In 1901, Spindletop, the first of the Texas oil-field gushers, was drilled and by 1915 United States production of petroleum was up to 281 million barrels. Starting with a multitude of individuals and small firms, the oil industry saw one company and one man emerge as the dominant power. This was the Standard Oil Company and the man was John D. Rockefeller, Sr. Standard Oil by 1904 controlled about 85 per cent of the domestic oil industry, including wells, refineries, pipelines, and marketing organizations. In fact, it was the first trust and the most complete monopoly. President Roosevelt ordered his attorney general to prosecute Standard Oil for violation of the Sherman Antitrust law. It was 1911 before the case reached the Supreme Court and the justices found that the oil firm was indeed a monopoly in restraint of trade. It ordered it broken up into a number of smaller companies. At the same time, though, the Court declared that it would apply its own "rule of reason" in each case, deciding whether in its opinion a particular monopoly was or was not doing harm to the public.

The Northern Securities case had its origin in a battle for financial control of several railroads, involving two of the toughest and shrewdest railroad men of the day and two of the most potent banking houses. On one side were Edward H. Harriman, successful not only as a financial manipulator of railroads but also as a constructive operator of them, and Jacob Schiff of the banking firm of Kuhn, Loeb and Company. Harriman controlled over 20,000 miles of rail lines, particularly the Union Pacific Railroad. On the opposite side were James J. Hill, who had built a railroad across Montana and on to Seattle, and J. P. Morgan, the head of his own firm of bankers. Hill controlled the Great Northern Railroad and the Northern Pacific. Each group decided in 1900 that it wanted to gain control of the Chicago, Burlington and Quincy Railroad because it ran into Chicago from the west. Hill succeeded in buying enough stock in 1901 to control the Burlington, leaving Harriman and his lines shut out from Chicago.

Harriman refused to accept defeat and decided to achieve his end in another way: he would buy control of the Northern Pacific before Hill knew what was happening and thereby gain dominance over the Burlington. When the Hill forces discovered what was up, they entered the market also, both sides trying to buy as much Northern Pacific stock as possible. Naturally, the price of Northern Pacific stock went up. In May, 1901, greedy speculators tried to get into the battle by selling the stock short. That is, they sold shares they did not possess, gambling that they could, by the required time, deliver such shares by acquiring them at a lower price from someone else. The stock went up in price from around $100 a share to $1,000. Those who had "borrowed" Northern Pacific stock and sold short now found they could not secure enough shares to make good. Complete disaster was imminent. Finally, the two banking firms let the frantic speculators settle for only $150 a share. The intense reaction to the frenzied speculation, by the newspapers and the public, sobered even the main participants. They agreed to form a new company, the Northern Securities Company, which would hold a majority of the stock of Hill's two railroads, would thus control the Burlington, and would include on its board of directors representatives of the Harriman-Schiff group as well as the majority Hill-Morgan group.

Early in 1902, Theodore Roosevelt, who had been president for only a few months, ordered the attorney general to start a suit under the Sherman Act, to dissolve the Northern Securities Company. This was a stunning blow to Wall Street, and especially to Morgan who thought he was entitled to treat with the United States government as an equal. Nevertheless, in 1904 the Supreme Court upheld the government and ordered Northern Securities dissolved.

The insurance business also came under suspicion about this time. Life insurance had become a big business and thousands of people paid millions of dollars a year in premiums. By 1904 the three largest firms had assets of almost $1,250,000,000. By controlling insurance companies, or by friendly arrangements with their officers, the bankers—such as J. P. Morgan—could in effect use the savings of thousands of Americans for their own purposes since the insurance companies had to invest their funds somewhere. They were also using some of their money to pay enormous salaries and commissions and to bribe politicians. An investigation in 1905–06 in New York, headed by Charles Evans Hughes, brought some of the shady doings to light and resulted in legislation that protected those who paid the money in premiums. Hughes found, for example, that James Hazen Hyde, son of the founder of Equitable Life and a great lover of French styles and manners, was paid $100,000 a year while still in his twenties and had also charged against the company an elaborate $12,000 dinner party he gave for the French ambassador.

The ultimate in trusts was the Money Trust. A small group of financiers and banks, it was charged, controlled most of the money and credit facilities of the country, and this power put all kinds of businesses and industries under the thumb of these bankers. A Congressional committee, headed by Representative Arsène Pujo, conducted a formal investigation and made its report in 1913. Yes, said the committee, if concentration of control of money creates a money trust, there was one. It pointed particularly at six banks and investment banking firms, and showed that officers and members of these organizations held in all 341 directorships in 112 corporations whose total value was $22,245,000,000. The Pujo Committee concluded that this small inside group was "more destructive of competition than anything accomplished by the trusts."

At the head of the committee's list of the six banking powers was J. P. Morgan and Company, and the star witness called before the hearings was J. P. Morgan himself, now seventy-five years old. He had greatly increased the size and wealth of the banking house his father had established, and had been especially successful in buying up and reorganizing railroads. His accumulated wealth and business power were matched by his dominating personality. His strong face was in turn dominated by an enormous purplish nose—which no one ever made fun of. At the hearing he tried to make light of his alleged power, and insisted to the end that so far as he was concerned, "a man I do not trust could not get money from me on all the bonds in Christendom." It was this utter self-confidence that made the other bankers defer to him. In private life he was a man of culture, who collected fabulous works of art and rare books which eventually were made available to the public. He also maintained an elaborate yacht named *Corsair*. Morgan died in 1913 and no one financier thereafter ever dominated the American economic world to the extent he had.

The meat packers, the food processors, and the drug and patent-medicine firms were also targets of the reformers and the antitrust forces. Both an official report and Upton Sinclair's novel, *The Jungle*, revolted people with their revelations of nauseating conditions prevailing in the Chicago packing houses. The result, with President Roosevelt's strong backing, was a Federal meat inspection law in 1906. That same year the first pure food and drug act was passed. This action was stimulated in part by a series of articles on patent medicines in 1905 in *Collier's* by Samuel Hopkins Adams, and by the campaign against adulterated food led by Dr. Harvey W. Wiley, chief chemist of the Department of Agriculture. The facts showed that preservatives and adulterants were being used almost universally in canned foods without the public being aware of it.

Whether in spite of or because of the power of the trusts and the financiers, there were two short but sharp financial panics, one in 1903 and one in 1907. Otherwise, on the whole the era from 1900 to World War I provided the nation with generally good times in economic affairs. There seemed to be no particular reason for the panic of 1903. Business and agriculture were operating at satisfactory levels, but the stock market went sharply down. Some businessmen tried to blame the trouble on President Roosevelt, overlooking the great glut of stocks and bonds being offered, much of which represented overcapitalization such as that of the United States Steel Corporation.

The panic of 1907 was more serious. It was due chiefly to overspeculation and to the unwise practices of trust companies which were not required to operate as conservatively as other kinds of banks. The crisis came in October when some banks, particularly the Knickerbocker Trust Company in New York, had to close their doors. The Federal government and leading capitalists combined to halt the collapse. J. P. Morgan called the important bankers to his palatial home in Manhattan and kept them there until they agreed to provide the financial support necessary to restore confidence in the banks. This action confined the trouble to a "rich man's panic," but still showed that the nation's banking system was not adequate for the times.

Meanwhile, American business at home and abroad was continuing to expand year by year. At the start of the century there were few large stores or chains. There were 200 Great Atlantic and Pacific Tea Company stores in 1900; by 1912 this number was doubled. Department stores were beginning to benefit by the growth of cities and by improved transportation. Ready-to-wear clothing and factory-made shoes were widely available and more acceptable to the public than in the past. Mail-order firms had been established in the nineteenth century and they, too, grew as the new century progressed. Sears, Roebuck and Company became the largest mail-order house in the world, with sales of more than $50,000,000 annually by 1907.

America's foreign trade was growing and changing, too. In 1900 the country exported goods worth about $1,500,000,000, and by the time war came this figure had increased by another billion dollars. At the same time, the nature of the exports was changing so that by 1912 less than half consisted of agricultural products. Meanwhile, Americans were also investing more money abroad, the total reaching about $3,500,000,000 by the start of World War I.

Scientific management and technological advances were important in the growth of the United States as an industrial nation in the world economy. Scientific management as a technique for increasing the efficiency of industrial production was not new in 1900, but it was in the next decade or so that it became a very considerable factor in the operation of manufacturing processes. In essence, scientific management meant the study and arrangement of the work of men and machines so as to achieve the most production at the least cost. The most active exponent of scientific management was Frederick W. Taylor (1856–1915). While still a young man, he had shown a talent for organizing work so as to increase the efficiency of both labor and machinery. He, and others like him, studied every motion a laborer made in the course of a day, timed these motions to the second, fitted men and machines together and increased production tremendously. In one classic example, Taylor told how he had retrained an ordinary laborer so that he could carry almost four times as much pig iron per day as he had previously.

The workers were suspicious of Taylor and his type of "efficiency expert." They believed they were being made to work harder and faster for the same money. No doubt some employers sought such a result. The scientific-management men, however, advocated higher pay for the men who learned by these methods to increase their production. They also advocated lower prices to consumers as costs were reduced. Certainly the system worked as far as increasing the efficiency of American industry was concerned.

At the same time, technological advances were accelerating the pace of industrial growth, and doing it so noticeably that newly devised machinery was one of the most popular exhibits at any national or international exposition. There were various indications of the prominent place science and technology were taking in the twentieth century: science fiction was becoming more popular; the California Institute of Technology was founded in 1901; nearly 1,000,000 patents were issued in the first quarter of the century. The urge for more and bigger and faster machines was spurred in the United States by the nation's chronic shortage of labor in relation to the size of the country and the economic opportunities it afforded. By 1900, 21 per cent of the American labor force was in manufacturing. In spite of industry's continued growth, machinery and processes were improved so rapidly that this percentage increased by only one point up to 1914. Of primary importance was the improvement of machine tools, spurred by the development of the harder carbon steel in 1900. Frederick W. Taylor was one of those whose research helped.

In 1900 coal was by far the most widely used source of energy. Electric power, which had been available commercially for about twenty years, provided only 10 per cent of the nation's energy requirements, but the use of it and of oil was increasing steadily. By 1905 most new factories were installing electric power to run their machines. The electric power industry, the developing internal combustion engine, and the almost entirely new chemical industry were the prime driving forces of economic change after 1900. Aluminum production, which depended on cheap electrical power, amounted to only 3,000 tons in 1900, but grew steadily thereafter. Magnesium could now be produced commercially also. Ammonia was first synthesized on a practical scale in 1912. The chemical industry increased threefold between 1900 and 1914. Bakelite came on the market in 1909 and the whole plastics industry grew from it. The General Electric Company established the first modern industrial-research laboratory in 1900 and other large manufacturing concerns soon followed suit.

Some of the great changes in the economic life of the United States came from discovery and invention, from technology and modern management. Changes also came from the way industry was financed, merged, and manipulated by those whose interest was in personal profit and control rather than the production of physical goods. Together, these changes presented the national government and the people with both problems and opportunities.

3 *Workers and Farmers*

THE ACCELERATING INDUSTRIALIZATION of the nation brought about profound changes in the relationship between labor and capital, employer and employee. Labor and management came into conflict more often and there were more and larger strikes. Labor sought not only to organize into unions, but also to secure its goals through politics and by state and Federal legislation. The employers, on the other hand, stepped up their efforts to crush the unions, either directly or through the legislatures and the courts.

The increasingly unequal distribution of wealth made those on the lower levels of the economic order want a larger share of the material things of life. Wages were low and hours were long. In 1900 the average workweek was about sixty hours, and the ten-hour day was common. In the steel industry many men worked a twelve-hour day and a seven-day week. The five-day week was nonexistent. In a few organized and skilled trades, men such as bricklayers, railroad engineers and plumbers made as much as $4 a day, but an unskilled laborer earned about $1.50. Girls who clerked in stores were paid $5 or $6 a week, and only a few workers earned as much as $18. Overall, the average annual earnings of all workers, except farm laborers, was only about $490 in 1900. Of course, prices were low also, so that comparison with today's wages and costs is difficult. Roast beef was about 15 cents a pound, milk 6 cents a quart, a good pair of men's heavy shoes $2.

A number of labor unions were started in the latter part of the nineteenth century, but by 1900 only one—the American Federation of Labor, which had been founded in 1886—could claim to be a national federation of unions representing many different trades. Its president and one of its founders was Samuel Gompers (1850–1924). Gompers was born in England and came to the United States as a boy, where he became a cigarmaker. Under his leadership the AFL achieved a membership of about 550,000 in 1900. It grew rapidly for a few years, reaching 1,600,000 members in 1905, but thereafter the rate of increase slowed. Membership was about 2,000,000 in 1914 and almost 2,500,000 in 1917.

From the start the AFL was a craft union, strongest with workers in the skilled trades. In this respect it was different from industrial unions where, as in the United Mine Workers, everyone in the industry belonged to the same union regardless of his particular skill.

The AFL and its early leaders favored immigration restriction, fearing that the thousands of unskilled laborers streaming in from Europe every year would flood the market with surplus workers willing to accept low rates of pay. Negroes were also quite effectively excluded from most AFL unions, partly because few had the necessary craft skills to qualify, but also in part simply from anti-Negro prejudice. The union that did more than any other to accept Negroes as members on the same terms as whites was the United Mine Workers, with 40,000 Negro members around 1910.

The AFL was not out to topple the capitalistic structure, but only to secure better wages, shorter hours and other practical goals for its own members. It advocated strikes to achieve these ends and it established union funds for pensions and illness. Some of its leaders at this time opposed state or Federal social welfare legislation on the grounds that it would weaken the unions if government provided these benefits for the workers. The leadership was also opposed to entering politics as a separate labor party. Instead, the AFL furthered its goals by endorsing individual candidates. Only in 1908 did it officially support one of the two major parties when it backed William Jennings Bryan and the Democrats. It seems certain, though, that workers, whether union members or not, tended to favor Democratic candidates.

A much more radical labor organization—and one that caused widespread controversy for a few years—was the Industrial Workers of the World, founded in 1905 and known popularly as the "Wobblies." It said forthrightly in its constitution that "the working class and the employing class have nothing in common." It sought to destroy the existing social system and establish in its place a "classless" society, but just how this was to be done was not clear. It was much more given to strong direct action than was the AFL, and the strikes it led were usually accompanied by violence. The IWW was strongest in the West among migratory workers, miners and lumbermen; in the East it picked up strength among textile-factory workers. The IWW organized a textile strike in Lawrence, Massachusetts, in 1912 and won it, but lost a similar strike in Paterson, New Jersey, in 1913. At about this same time the IWW reached its peak membership of 100,000.

The IWW's best-known leader was the colorful William D. (Big Bill) Haywood (1869–1928), a handsome, one-eyed man who was an advocate of sabotage and mass action. In 1907, in a trial that attracted nationwide attention, Haywood was tried as an accessory in the murder of former Governor Frank Steunenberg of Idaho. Presumably Steunenberg had been killed by radical labor elements because he had asked for Federal troops in a labor dispute. Haywood was acquitted. When the United States entered World War I, Haywood and other leaders of the IWW showed their opposition by word and deed. Haywood was tried for sedition and convicted, but fled to Russia before he could be locked up to serve his term. These events destroyed the IWW for all practical purposes.

The struggle to organize labor also had a direct bearing on the form socialism took in the United States in the early years of the century. One of the most energetic young labor leaders of the late nineteenth century was the Indiana-born Eugene V. Debs (1855–1926), who first became a leader among railway workers. A term in jail for violating a court's antistrike injunction led him to socialism through the books he read while serving his sentence. He was one of the early leaders of the IWW, but broke with that organization because he believed the way to socialism and the betterment of the laboring man was through political action. For twenty years he was the Socialist Party's candidate for the presidency, reaching a high of 900,000 votes in 1912.

As unions tried harder to organize more plants and more industries, and as management began to battle unionism, larger and fiercer strikes were inevitable. Union leaders considered a closed shop essential to their efforts, while the employers, led by the National Association of Manufacturers, realized that if management could continue the open shop, where union membership was not required, organized labor could never become very strong. Unorganized immigrant labor could be brought in to replace strikers. The first significant strike of the century came in 1901 against the newly organized industrial giant, the United States Steel Corporation. Over 60,000 men went on strike under the leadership of the Amalgamated Association of Iron, Steel and Tin Workers. The union, however, was able to hold out for only about two months and had to accept terms that admitted defeat. Eight years later United States Steel decided to be done with the union entirely and declared all its mills open shops. The union called a strike that went on for fourteen months but it was totally defeated.

The first strike in which a president of the United States intervened to bring about a settlement began in May, 1902, when the

United Mine Workers struck in the anthracite coalfield of Pennsylvania. Most of the mines were owned by half-a-dozen railroads, and their presidents all refused to enter into any kind of negotiations. Their arrogant and obstinate attitude lost them all public sympathy, and even many conservative newspapers and politicians denounced them. Finally, President Roosevelt called both sides to a meeting in Washington in early October. By this time winter was approaching and coal was getting scarce and expensive. Since schools, businesses and homes all depended primarily on hard coal for heat, the strike affected nearly everyone. Roosevelt again proposed arbitration and the union leader, John F. Mitchell, again agreed. Once more, though, the mine owners refused and their spokesmen went out of their way to insult Mitchell. Roosevelt was furious and, while admitting that he had no particular legal power to do anything, prepared to send Army units to the coalfields to take over the mines if necessary. He also discussed the problem with other influential persons, and indirectly with J. P. Morgan who helped bring the owners around to a reasonable attitude. A commission was appointed by the President and when it reported in March, 1903, it gave the mine workers a 10 per cent raise and reduced working hours, but did not grant the union official recognition.

Colorado was the scene of two bitter miners' strikes in this period. Trouble broke out in 1903 when the miners struck at Cripple Creek. The Governor, entirely on the owners' side, called out the militia, and in effect ordered them to destroy the union's organization. Ten years later, when an attempt was made to unionize the Colorado Fuel and Iron Company, even more violence resulted. Armed guards hired by the company and state militia harassed the strikers and brought about a pitched battle between miners and soldiers. President Wilson, who had been trying to get the two sides to come to terms, finally ordered in Federal troops. This was the first time troops were used not to protect the employers' property and to put down the strikers, but to protect the property and persons of both sides impartially.

Labor also battled for legal recognition and protection by way of the courts and the legislatures, but had little success for some years. One early victory was achieved in 1908 when the Supreme Court upheld an Oregon law that limited the daily hours of employment for women to ten. The case was also notable because the justices considered sociological, economic and physiological data, as well as legal, in reaching their decision. However, when it came to laws concerning unions and laboring men, the courts in general handed down restrictive decisions. A New York State law in 1897 made it illegal for a bakery to allow an employee to work more than ten hours a day or sixty hours a week. But in 1905, when a test case reached the Supreme Court, the law was declared unconstitutional by five to four, by the narrowest of margins. The justices held it violated the Fourteenth Amendment to the Constitution. In effect, this was saying that the law denied an individual the "right" to work as many hours a week as he pleased.

The actions of labor unions were severely restricted by two other test cases. These concerned attempts by unions to force concessions from employers by boycotting their products. The Bucks' Stove and Range Company in 1907 secured an injunction against Samuel Gompers and others because the American Federation of Labor had put the company on an "unfair list." In 1908 the Supreme Court upheld, under the Sherman Act, a prosecution of a union that had boycotted a firm of hatters in Danbury, Connecticut. The individual members of the union were held responsible for losses sustained by the business as a result of the boycott.

Labor hoped and believed that its basic problem of legality was settled in its favor in 1914 when the Clayton Antitrust Act became law. This law, part of President Wilson's campaign against monopoly, included with his blessing a section that declared labor unions and farmers' organizations were not, as such, conspiracies in restraint of trade—which was the way they had been treated under the Sherman Act. "The labor of a human being," the new law declared, "is not a commodity or article of commerce." But the terms of this part of the law were general and vague enough so that conservative courts in the next few years found little difficulty in penalizing unions for various activities.

Nevertheless, efforts to pass social welfare legislation, especially at the state level, continued. Through the work of unions and of the progressives, more such laws came into effect, although the United States long lagged behind several Western European countries. The first minimum-wage law for women was enacted by Massachusetts in 1902. By 1917 about a third of the states had such laws. Union officials at first opposed the idea of minimum-wage laws for fear the minimum would become the maximum, but gradually they withdrew their opposition, especially where women and children were concerned.

The problem of child labor was one that drew particular attention. About 1,750,000 children from ten to fifteen years of age were gainfully employed in 1900, most of them in farming. A book published in 1906, *The Bitter Cry of the Children,* by John Spargo, who was active in the reform movement, gave impetus to the drive to end child labor. He revealed some shocking figures: 20,000 children under twelve were working in southern cotton mills in 1902; 25,000 boys in 1900 were employed in or around the nation's mines and quarries, a "breaker boy" received 60 cents for a ten-hour day. In West Virginia it was legal to employ in the mines, day or night, for any number of hours, boys twelve years of age. Gradually the states began to try to control child labor. In 1916 a Federal law was passed to regulate child labor in industries involved in interstate commerce, but this was declared unconstitutional two years later by the Supreme Court. The problems of child labor and school attendance were closely related. At the start of the century only seven states required school attendance to the age of sixteen. By 1915 the number increased to thirty-three.

The United States was the last of the industrial nations to force companies to take responsibility for accidents suffered by their workmen. Maryland in 1902 passed a workmen's compensation act and was followed by other states. Maryland's law and those of some other states met the same fate as did so much other social welfare legislation: they were held unconstitutional. After 1911 the states drafted laws that the courts approved.

While labor was making progress slowly and painfully, agriculture was somewhat better off. Mechanization and scientific methods greatly increased the productivity of the nation's farms. On the whole, the period from the beginning of the century to the end of World War I was a good one for farmers, although it was not without its problems. On the one hand, the great increase in the quantity of farm products made it necessary to compete in world markets with the agricultural produce of other countries. On the other hand, the farmer as an independent, individual producer could not control output and prices the way the manufacturing monopolies could. The farmer, therefore, complained loudly about the prices he had to pay for manufactured products—many of them protected by a high tariff—and about the arbitrary freight rates charged him by the railroads on whom he depended for transporting his goods to market.

In spite of having more farm land in use, and producing larger crops than ever, a much smaller proportion of the country's inhabitants were living on farms because manufacturing and the service trades grew greatly in this period. About nine out of every ten workers were farmers in 1800; a hundred years later only one in three, and the trend continued. Meanwhile the value of farms and equipment went up. While in 1900 farmers owned $750,000,000 worth of machinery and equipment, by 1920 this figure was over $3,500,000,-

000. The total value of all farm property in 1900, when there were 6,000,000 farms, was a little over $20,000,000,000; ten years later the value had doubled.

The increase in productivity and value, as well as the decrease in the number of farmers, were directly attributable to science and technology. The horse was the standard source of power on the farm in 1900, and as late as 1917 there were 28,000,000 horses and mules in the country, but after that came a rapid decline. The steam engine was providing a good deal of power and its use reached a peak about 1910. At that time there were 100,000 self-propelled steam engines doing a variety of chores on farms. The gasoline engine then began quite rapidly to become the main source of farmers' power. The soon-to-be familiar tractor led the way. In 1907 there were only 600 of them, but by 1917 the number had increased to 90,000. The effect of mechanization can be summed up in one sample figure: in 1800 it took 344 man-hours of work to produce 100 bushels of corn; by 1910 the same amount required only 147 man-hours.

The internal combustion engine when applied to the automobile did as much as anything to revolutionize farm life. It not only carried farm produce to the nearest railroad, but it also carried the farmer and his family into town and ended the isolation of the farm home. Electric power, on the other hand, did not bring its benefits to the countryside until relatively late. While some farmers put in their own power plants, as late as 1919 only 100,000 farms were connected to the lines of private utility companies which did not think it profitable to extend them further.

4 *Transportation and Communication*

AN INDUSTRIAL AND URBAN NATION, such as the United States had become by the twentieth century, could not exist as a unity over its continent-wide expanse without transportation and communication facilities to match. Fortunately, it already had the most extensive railroad network in the world and new methods of urban transportation were in view. The automobile was in its infancy and its use was about to grow rapidly. The airplane was not yet invented, although man soon would achieve powered flight. The telephone was already in practical use and its wires were creeping steadily over the land. Wireless was in its experimental stage, but ready to link continents and ships with the shore.

The American railroad system dominated transportation. There was no other fast and economical way to carry large quantities of bulky and heavy materials from one part of the country to another. American railroads constituted one of the biggest business enterprises in the world with $10,000,000,000 worth of property in 1900. This amounted to a tenth of all the wealth of the country. At the end of the Civil War there were 35,000 miles of railroad tracks, but by 1900 there were 198,000 miles. More miles of tracks continued to be built, although at a slower rate. An all-time high in total track mileage was reached in 1916, 254,000 miles. After that, although some rail lines were built, more were abandoned. Also in 1916, the railroads were carrying 77 per cent of all intercity freight traffic and 98 per cent of intercity passenger business. Most other traffic was carried by ships on the Great Lakes and on rivers and canals.

The railroad system was one of the largest employers, too. Just over a million persons worked for the rails in 1900 and nearly a million and three quarters in 1916. Railroad employment reached its peak in 1920, at 2,000,000, and then declined, partly because of increased operating efficiency and partly because of the growing competition of the auto, truck and bus.

Almost all railroad locomotives were powered by steam, and technological development continued to increase their capacity. One of these developments was superheating, by which the temperature of the steam was increased and its condition changed from moist to dry. Trains became longer and heavier, speeds were higher. There was some electrification of railroads, mainly in areas with tunnels or in urban districts. Steel cars for both freight and passenger use were just coming in at the start of the century and the first all-steel Pullman went into service in 1907. Larger and handsomer rail terminals were built in the cities.

Despite the impressive performance of American railroads as examples of modern technology, and despite the fact that they were an absolute necessity to the nation, no industry and no group of owners and managers were so hated by millions of people. No one was to blame except the railroad owners themselves. The rails had a position so dominating in the economic life of the nation that it is hard to imagine the situation now. Attempts to control them by legislation had mostly failed, and a railroad could, by arbitrarily raising or lowering its rates, doom one town or area in favor of another. Judges and members of legislatures were bribed, or received gifts and privileges that amounted to bribes. One of the most notorious evils was the open-handed distribution of free passes to public-office holders and other influential people. Those who controlled the roads were as arrogant a group in disregard of the public interest as any in the country's history.

Another cause of public resentment was the way in which railroads were used by speculators to reap fortunes in stock manipulation at the expense of the good of the railroad lines as a transportation industry. The insiders carried out "raids" and formed "pools" by which they bought enough stock to control a particular line. They had no interest in operating the road in most cases, but there were millions to be gained by issuing more stocks and bonds than were justified by the railroad's physical properties. Or a road might have a cash surplus in its treasury which soon disappeared into the pockets of the new controllers. The Chicago and Alton Railroad was the victim of a raid of this kind between 1898 and 1905. George J. Gould, son of the even more rapacious railroad looter, Jay Gould, and James Stillman, of the National City Bank in New York, were the leaders of a group that got control of this road, expanded its capitalization by about $80,000,000 and pocketed at least $23,000,000 for themselves. Another group, headed by William H. Moore, used borrowed money in the amount of only $5,000,000 and a system of exchanging securities between holding companies to get control of the Rock Island Railroad and of a rail system whose capital structure came to $1,500,000,000.

In the twentieth century most of the financial manipulation of railroad property stemmed from the attempts of various persons and groups to merge individual railroad lines into large regional alignments. About two-thirds of all the rail mileage existing in 1906 was controlled by seven groups. There were the Vanderbilt roads, the Pennsylvania system, the Morgan roads, the Gould roads, the Rock Island System, the Hill roads and the Harriman roads. In actuality, even the nominal heads of these powerful concentrations were not the bosses because the bankers, especially such houses as J. P. Morgan and Company and Kuhn, Loeb and Company, held the real purse strings. Except for those who suffered personal loss, the disaster that befell J. P. Morgan when he tried to achieve a monopoly on all transportation in New England was well-deserved. Working through the New York, New Haven and Hartford Railroad, Morgan paid fantastic prices for other properties, including shipping and trolley systems as well as railroads. The end result was the financial ruin of the New Haven.

Considering the key position occupied by the railroads and the way in which they flouted public opinion, it is hardly surprising that there were demands for state and Federal regulation. In the nineteenth century this campaign was led by the farmers of the West and South. The agitation became part of the general antitrust movement, and was a cause of the progressives also. Congress had created the Interstate Commerce Commission and while the Commission had certain powers, it could not set rates. The railroads fought its actions at every turn, and the courts helped keep it feeble.

President Roosevelt took the lead in 1905 in demanding more regulation of the roads and the result the next year was the Hepburn Act. This law increased the powers of the Interstate Commerce Commission which had been established in 1887. As first organized, the Commission could investigate railroads and their policies, but it could not set rates for carrying goods and passengers. The Hepburn Act gave the ICC this authority, and it strengthened the rules forbidding roads to give rebates to favored shippers. President Taft also sought legislation to regulate the carriers and the result was the Mann-Elkins Act of 1910. This law extended the ICC's jurisdiction to telephone, telegraph and cable companies. As to the railroads, it prohibited them from charging more for a short haul than for a long one over the same route. Under President Wilson in 1916 the Adamson Act was passed which established an eight-hour day for railroad workers. The act was precipitated by a threatened strike of the railroad unions at a time when defense preparations were creating heavy freight traffic. It had the effect of setting a general standard sought by many unions.

Transportation developments of the period were also closely linked to the growth of the population and its increasing concentration in large cities. The larger a city, the more and better transportation facilities were necessary; and the better the transportation system, the more people could and did live in the metropolitan areas. The steam railroad made commuting from the suburbs possible, although until the coming of the automobile only those who could afford a carriage and driver could live beyond walking distance of the station.

The steam-railroad system was applied to cities by building elevated tracks for trains, and at the start of the century New York, Chicago and a few other large cities had elevated railroads. They were, however, extremely unpopular because of the noise and dirt they created, and they were soon converted to electrical operation. Meanwhile, the electric trolley was rapidly replacing the horse car as the chief means of city transportation. By 1902 almost all streetcars were electrically operated; less than 300 miles were operated with horsepower, and more than 20,000 miles were electrically powered. This newly applied source of power also made it possible to utilize subways and thus provide cities with an even faster means of transportation. Boston had a short subway line, using ordinary trolley cars, before 1900, but the first real American subway system was begun in New York in 1900. It was opened in 1904 and ran from Brooklyn Bridge uptown to 145th Street. The subway system was soon lengthened, including tunnels under the East River between Manhattan and Brooklyn.

The electric trolley systems were further extended to provide transportation between neighboring cities and towns. They spread so that around 1914 one could travel from New York to Boston, or from Chicago to Utica, New York, by these interurban trolleys, but it took a good deal of time and patience, for one had to transfer many times. Frederick Lewis Allen in *The Big Change* (Harper & Brothers, 1952) asks:

> Who remembers, now, such bright flowers of the streetcar era as the "Berkshire Hills", the extra-fare interurban trolley car that ran between Great Barrington, Massachusetts, and Bennington, Vermont, for several years after 1908—an elegant white car with buff trim and gold-leaf lettering, with wicker seats inside, and red brocaded curtains, and a Wilton carpet, all at the traveler's disposal for an extra fare of fifty cents?

The interurban trolleys were particularly popular because many of them, at the end of the line, left the passenger at an amusement park and picnic grounds, often operated by the same company that ran the cars. In the early years of the new century one of the favorite pastimes was to take a Sunday or holiday ride, with a picnic basket, to one of these amusement centers where one could ride on the merry-go-round and the roller coaster. On some excursions the cars were gaily lighted at night and there was a small band aboard. These adventures were a boon at little cost for the people who were otherwise restricted to the crowded city. Such excursions became so popular that they were denounced by clergymen who saw church attendance drop, and there was even one prediction that the interurban trolley would bring to an end the reading of books.

By comparison with developments on land and in the air, the story of shipping in the pre-World War I period is dull. American shipping was of no consequence outside our own lakes, rivers and canals, and beyond our own coastal waterways. Around 1800 American ships had carried nine-tenths of the nation's foreign trade, but by 1900 less than 10 per cent was being transported in American-owned freighters. There were no great profits to be made in shipping compared with other businesses, and United States ships were not subsidized by the government as were those of other important maritime nations. For passengers, it was an era of bigger and more luxurious ships which competed for the trade of well-to-do travelers and for the Atlantic-crossing speed record. The fastest passenger liner afloat in 1900 was the German *Deutschland.* Then in 1907 the British launched the *Lusitania* and the *Mauritania.* The former set a new record on her maiden voyage to New York and then broke it a few weeks later, crossing the Atlantic in about an hour and a quarter under five days. The *Mauritania* took the blue ribbon away from the *Lusitania* and held it until 1929.

The most important development in transportation in the period, both in its effect on the economy of the nation and on the life of the individual citizen, was the amazing rise of the gasoline-powered automobile. The "horseless carriage" was invented before the century began, and a number of people in the United States and Europe can claim some of the credit. It was in the early years of the century, though, that American inventors, engineers, manufacturers and salesmen turned the new means of transportation into a practical convenience that verged on becoming a necessity for every family.

The first automobiles looked exactly like carriages without horses. Some of them, in fact, had sockets for holding whips. Steering for a while was by a tiller rather than a wheel. For a few years there was competition among electric-powered, steam-powered and gasoline-driven cars. In the gasoline category the air-cooled and water-cooled engines competed until the latter won out. By 1910 most cars offered four-cylinder engines, and in 1915 the luxurious Packard boasted a twelve-cylinder power plant. The steering wheel was shifted from the right to left side about 1910, where it has remained ever since in the United States. Until about 1912 cars had to be cranked by hand. Then the self-starter was developed. This not only made life easier for men, but also meant that women could now operate motor vehicles without a man being on hand to crank. The rubber industry developed better pneumatic tires in a day when many motorists put patches on their tires themselves and pumped them up with hand pumps. The oil industry began to thrive as the growing number of autos burned up increasing quantities of gasoline. Many motorists carried a spare can of gas because in those days gas pumps were far apart.

At first automobiles were playthings for the mechanically minded and for the well-to-do. Hundreds of different men and small companies produced cars, and there were scores of makes. Most of the names of these early cars have disappeared and only a handful have survived. There was the Apperson, and the Franklin (air-cooled), and the Pierce Arrow, and the Locomobile. Before too long a few men and a few companies began to organize the auto industry on a practical basis.

Henry Ford (1863–1947), a Michigan farm boy, was attracted early to tinkering with horseless carriages, and in 1903 formed the Ford Motor Company. He soon realized that if he was going to be able to sell autos in quantity he had to first design a reliable, simple car. The next step was to produce it in sufficient quantities so that the price could be brought down within the reach of a mass market. This he accomplished when he introduced in 1908 the Model-T, the famous "tin lizzie," a four-cylinder, ten-horsepower car. In 1913 he began to experiment with the assembly-line technique and extended it the following year. Parts for Fords were brought to a moving production line and each worker put some small part of the finished product together as it went by him. That same year, 1914, Ford astounded the world by paying his factory workers $5 a day, which was about double the going rate.

In the first year of the "tin lizzie," fewer than 6,000 of them were produced and the touring car, most common model of the time, sold for $850. By 1916 more than half a million Model-T's were sold and the price had come down to $360. Ford's methods were adopted by others and the day of the individual automobile manufacturer operating out of a tool shed was over. General Motors, which eventually was to dominate the industry, was formed in 1908 and began to gather together the makers of such cars as Buick, Oldsmobile and Chevrolet. At this time Michigan was already becoming the center of the auto industry. About 4,000 new cars were manufactured in 1900, about 187,000 were produced in 1910, nearly a million in 1915, and 2,227,349 in 1920, by which time more than 9,000,000 cars, trucks and buses were operating on the streets and highways of the nation.

In the early days, when automobile owning and driving was a sport rather than a practical matter, a day on the road was an adventure. The occupants of a car with open sides, and often no top, had to be well protected with linen dusters and goggles, while women had to tie down their hats with veils that went under the chin. Racing stars, such as Barney Oldfield, were well known. The wealthy William K. Vanderbilt, Jr., whose garages were said to be able to hold a hundred cars and who employed twenty mechanics, beginning in 1904 sponsored an annual race on Long Island that was both a social event of the first order and a noisy and dangerous experience for onlookers. The first auto trips across the American continent were made in 1903, requiring about two months to complete. There were many competitions of this kind, called road tests, and the most exciting of all was the New York-to-Paris race in 1908. Cars of several different nations undertook the test, driving across the United States, then traveling by sea to Siberia, and driving on to Paris. An American car won, making the journey in about five and a half months.

Such tests, as well as ordinary driving nearer home, made clear that the auto could expand its role only to the extent that roads were improved. Pressure from motorists and business interests caused local governments to take some first steps, and in 1913 a Lincoln Highway Association was formed to promote a coast-to-coast highway. The first Federal aid to highways was voted in 1916 when Congress approved a law based on the assumption that highway improvement was needed primarily to help the farmer get to market.

When he was president of Princeton University, in 1906, Woodrow Wilson worried about the motor car, asserting that "nothing has spread socialistic feeling in this country more than the use of the automobile," adding that "to the countryman they are a picture of arrogance and wealth, with all its independence and carelessness." Seven years later, Wilson became the first president of the United States to ride to his inauguration in an auto. And when war came in 1917, he called on the automobile industry to produce not only cars and trucks, but also other equipment that its assembly line technique made possible.

Man's age-old dream of powered and controlled flight in a heavier-than-air machine came true in 1903, but aviation was of little practical value, except in warfare, until well after the progressive era. Many men had tried to conquer the air but the victory finally went to a pair of skillful mechanics from Dayton, Ohio. They used the facilities of their bicycle repair shop and factory to devise ways of controlling in the air the flight of a biplane whose wings were cloth-covered. They also built their own engine. They were two brothers, Wilbur (1867–1912) and Orville Wright (1871–1948). At Kitty Hawk, North Carolina, on December 17, 1903, they got their plane off the ground four times. Orville had the honor of making the first controlled flight in a power-driven plane. He stayed up for twelve seconds. On the fourth flight that day Wilbur stayed up for fifty-nine seconds and covered 859 feet.

Their epochal feat received almost no attention and most newspapers, deluded by such reports before, scoffed at or ignored the event. It was five years before they got much recognition, and that came first in France. Not until 1909 was the United States Army ready to buy its first Wright-built plane for military use.

Other pioneer flyers and designers were also active. Glenn H. Curtiss (1878–1930) in 1910 made a spectacular flight from Albany to New York City and won a $10,000 prize. Two years later he developed a hydroplane, or "flying boat." A French aviator, Louis Blériot, in 1909 was the first to fly a plane across the English Channel. In 1911 a plane set a new altitude record of 11,642 feet and that same year Calbraith P. Rodgers was the first to fly across the continent from New York to Long Beach, California. It took him forty-nine days, of which eighty-two hours and four minutes were actual flying-time. He survived nineteen crashes on the way. The St. Petersburg–Tampa Air Boat Line, which went into business early in 1914, was the first passenger-carrying airline in the United States.

On the whole, airplanes were more of a novelty than a practical means of transportation until World War I. Most of the flying was of an experimental nature, or else it was stunt flying, such as skimming low under a bridge. War gave great impetus to the development of aviation. The airplane's value for observation and reconnaissance was quickly realized. In turn, means of arming planes had to be devised to attack the enemy's observation planes, or to protect one's own. The final step was to carry small bombs and drop them, by hand, on enemy targets.

Great changes were taking place in communication as well as in transportation. The telephone, already a quarter of a century old, was becoming a necessity in business, although it was still a strange and terrifying instrument to many housewives. There were about 1,500,000 phones in use in 1900, and the American Telephone and Telegraph Company was already capitalized at a quarter of a billion dollars. By 1915 the number of phones had increased to more than 9,000,000. That same year several milestones were passed: the first transcontinental phone line between New York and San Francisco was opened; the first phone call was made from a moving train; and the first voice transmission between the United States and Paris took place, although it was a dozen years before this communication link became practical. The United States was on its way to being the talkingest nation in the world.

Communication by electric impulses sent through the air without the benefit of wires was even newer than the telephone. The primary inventor, Guglielmo Marconi (1874–1937), an Italian, had demonstrated the practicality of wireless telegraphy as early as 1895. In December, 1901, he succeeded in establishing the first trans-Atlantic wireless link. A station in England transmitted the letter "S" in Morse code to Newfoundland. In 1909 Marconi was awarded a Nobel Prize in physics. The wireless was first viewed as being useful chiefly for communication between ships and the shore, and ships were soon equipped with Marconi's instruments. As time went on many lives were saved by such ships' ability to let others know if anything went wrong. President Roosevelt sent a Morse code message of greeting to King Edward VII of England in January, 1903, and received a reply. In 1905 the world learned quickly by wireless of the battle of Port Arthur in Asia during the Russo-Japanese War.

Even this early other inventors and engineers were attracted to a still more dazzling goal: the transmission of the human voice and music through space, not just the dots and dashes of the telegrapher. Among pioneers in this field were Lee DeForest (1873–1961) and Reginald A. Fessenden (1866–1932). Many experimental broadcasts were made, such as that of Fessenden on Christmas Eve, 1906, when he contributed a violin solo. Although radio broadcasting played no part in the entertainment of the nation until the 1920's, wireless telegraphy and radio telephony, like the automobile and the airplane, were taken up by the military and used effectively in World War I.

The early years of the twentieth century were a period of transition in travel and communication. The dominance of the horse and the railroad was coming to an end. The automobile was taking a major place in the field and the airplane was born. And just as travel was getting faster and more convenient, it was becoming possible to send one's voice almost anywhere instead of making the trip oneself.

5 *New Cities and New Citizens*

THE MODERN CITY is the product of the Industrial Revolution and of the steady growth of the population. In England, where the Industrial Revolution began, a pattern was set that appeared later in other countries. The change in economic life both drew and forced rural inhabitants into the industrial towns. In the United States this movement from country to city, and from an agricultural to an industrial civilization, was further complicated by the enormous influx of immigrants. American cities had to cope with two kinds of persons, rural natives and foreign newcomers. They were very different, and were often suspicious of each other. A further complication was that most of the immigrants from Europe were from rural areas, too, so that they had the double problem of coping with a strange land and language, and with city life.

The new industrial city was not just a larger version of the county seat of a rural area. It was a different kind of place with bigger and different problems. Neighbor no longer knew neighbor, and new ties of friends and families had to be established in the unfamiliar environment. Rapid mass transportation was necessary for many could no longer walk to work. There was not only more garbage to dispose of, but it also had to be taken farther to get rid of it. A criminal could disappear much more easily in the crowded tenements of a slum than in a village.

The modern cities were the center of social and intellectual change and so they drew the young, the bright and the ambitious. They were also, in the eyes of the farm dwellers, the centers of sin and everything that was wrong with the machine age. Many a rural office-holder made political hay by denouncing the sinful city and promising a return to "the American way" of life. Life in the cities also spotlighted the increasing gulf between the rich and the poor. On the one hand there were the mansions, the jewels, and the elaborate parties of the rich, most of whom had had money for only a short time and were not yet familiar with the more refined ways of spending it. On the other hand there were the very poor, mostly recent arrivals from overseas. They were helpless in the hands of the landlords who exploited them through high rents in tenement houses and employers who offered miserable pay for long hard hours of work.

Nevertheless, the metropolis was an actuality. More and more people had to live in it, and much as some of them may have cried out at the harshness of life in the new cities, they stayed there. Additional thousands joined them every year. New York City had almost 3,500,000 inhabitants in 1900; by 1910 the figure approached 5,000,000 and New York was one of the great cities of the world. Chicago had already become the second largest city in the nation in 1900 with 1,500,000 residents; by 1910 it passed the 2,000,000 mark. The older Eastern cities, Boston, Philadelphia and Baltimore, grew too, but not nearly as fast as the rapidly rising cities of the Midwest, such as Cleveland, Detroit and St. Louis.

These twentieth-century cities didn't deal effectively with their new problems. Miles of streets needed to be paved, much more water was necessary to supply the people of the city, many more school buildings were called for. Who was to see that all these things were done? The machinery of municipal government, inherited from a less hurried era, was not adapted to running what amounted to a number of complicated business enterprises providing services to millions of people. Here was temptation for those who wanted to get control of the municipal governing machinery and for those who saw large profits to be made in supplying essential services.

Most of those who went into politics were not civic-minded men eager to serve the public. They often came from one of the older immigrant groups such as the Irish, because politics was one of the few enticing paths to power and money that was open to them. There was, for example, George Washington Plunkitt who went from a butcher's shop to a place of influence in Tammany Hall, the Democratic political machine in New York. He made a good deal of money from what he called "honest graft," because, as he said, "I seen my opportunities and I took 'em." On the other hand, it is only fair to point out that in this era two future political leaders of great stature got their start in public life through Tammany Hall. They were Alfred E. Smith, who became governor of New York State and Democratic candidate for the presidency, and Robert F. Wagner, Sr., a leading United States senator in the 1930's.

The Plunkitt kind of politician got his votes by doing favors for the poor and ignorant. He made his money by taking bribes ("boodle") from the successful, and often well-born, businessmen. There was great competition for franchises and contracts to supply the cities with transportation, with gas, with paving materials, and everything else that they needed. Businessmen paid politicians for the privileges, as the muckrakers made known. Some of the best fictionalized accounts of this process are in Theodore Dreiser's *The Financier* and *The Titan.*

There soon was a growing reaction against the looting of city treasuries and the inefficiency and high cost of municipal services. Honesty in government became one of the rallying cries of the progressives. In a number of cities at different times—New York, Cleveland and Detroit, for example—reform movements carried the day and officials pledged to honesty were elected. In some cases, while this put an end to corruption for a while, it did not bring in officials really able to cope with the practical side of managing the city services. The reform movement was strongly in favor of municipal ownership of utilities, although this did not stem from a belief in the theories of socialism. The reformers thought they could prove how much cheaper and more efficiently gas, electricity and water could be supplied if the tempting relationship between utilities and politicians was severed. Thus a number of cities in this period became owners of public service industries.

New forms of city government were also advocated and experimented with. These were based on the proposition that municipal government was a business, a service unit for citizens, not a matter of partisan politics such as seemed appropriate on the national level. One popular new system was the commission form of government. In this a small elected commission, one of whose members was chosen mayor, replaced the separately elected mayor with wide powers and the large body of legislators, usually called aldermen. It turned out, though, that this plan did not always eliminate politics. The city manager idea was also advocated. In this system, the city's governing body hired an expert who ran the various city departments and services. The city manager system was first tried in Staunton, Virginia, in 1908.

Cities had many practical matters to deal with in a time of growth and change. One of them was street paving. Cobblestones, granite blocks, wooden blocks and bricks had all been used in different parts of the country. Now asphalt was used more extensively and easily, but even in 1900 two-thirds of all Chicago's streets were not paved at all. Electricity was already being used to light city streets, although there were still many gas lamps. Street cleaning was a neglected art. Many streets were never cleaned and America lagged behind the European cities in this respect and in the matter of collecting and disposing of garbage. However, the germ theory of disease was beginning to be accepted and agitation was growing for better sanitary conditions as far as garbage disposal and water supply were concerned. The overall death rate in the cities was higher than in the country, but gradually the urban rate began to improve. New York City in 1900 had 5,000 street cleaners and garbage collectors, and its commissioner of street cleaning introduced quick snow removal after storms. New York's and Boston's fire departments were quite likely the best in the world, while Chicago had as many firemen and more engines and horses than did London.

Housing for the poorer classes was the worst problem of all, and one about which city governments did very little for many years. It was not considered the duty of the city to build public housing, and there were selfish interests fighting any regulation of the slum tenements from which much money was made. The thousands of persons from the countryside and from Europe who were pouring into the cities had little money and hence little choice in living accommodations, which were always at a premium because of the continued growth of the population.

At the start of the century the dumbell-shaped tenement dominated slum housing in New York City. Shaped as its name implied, it covered almost all the land area and allowed the landlord to crowd four families onto each floor. With ten such tenements on a block there might be as many as 4,000 people living in that small an area. In 1900 there were 42,700 buildings in New York classed as tenements, and they housed more than 1,500,000 people. At a hearing on the slum problem in New York in 1900 one witness who had lived most of his life in tenement houses testified:

> . . . the air shaft is a breeder of disease and . . . there can be no fresh air in any building with an air shaft, from my experience, because of the refuse thrown down in the air shaft, the stench is so vile and the air is so foul that the occupants do not employ the windows as a means of getting air. . . . Because there are no baths

> in the tenement houses many of the tenants do not bathe as often as they otherwise would. I can say from experience that many tenants do not bathe more than six times a year, and often less. . . .

The report of the commission which heard such testimony led to an improved code. It required that all rooms and hallways be ventilated and lighted. It imposed strict rules concerning running water, sanitation, the size of rooms, and fire protection. Other states and cities followed New York's lead and by 1910 the housing situation was improved, but far from ideal.

The growth in numbers of the American people and their spread over the continent was in large part due to immigration, which was sizable even before the Civil War. By 1900 there were more than 10,000,000 persons of foreign birth and 26,000,000 who were children of immigrants in the United States. The largest number to come in one year was 1,285,349 in 1907, while 1914 was next with 1,218,420. The decade 1901–10 set a record with 8,795,386 newcomers, followed by the 1911–20 decade with 5,735,811, so that a total of more than 14,500,000 persons arrived in the twenty-year period. Most could not speak English, many could not read or write, and most were entirely unfamiliar with the ways of America and with its English heritage.

Until near the end of the nineteenth century the majority of the immigrants came from Western and Northern Europe—Great Britain, Germany and Scandinavia especially. While many of these people, especially the Irish, settled in the cities, a good number went west to take up farming. Now the new immigrants were coming chiefly from Southern and Eastern Europe, especially from Russia, Poland, Austria-Hungary and Italy. They were less able to fit into American life in a short time. Most of them were peasants but they could not easily become American farmers: they did not have the capital, nor the knowledge of American conditions, nor were there any longer millions of acres of rich farmland to be had for the taking.

Consequently, they stayed for the most part in the cities, and they stayed among their own kind. This made assimilation all the more difficult. By 1900, 86 per cent of the foreign born lived in the area north of the Ohio River and east of the Mississippi River. In New York City and in Chicago, three-quarters of the inhabitants were foreign born or the children of foreign born. Taking America's twelve largest cities as a group, 60 per cent of the population fell into one or the other of these categories. The bosses of America's expanding industries welcomed this new supply of cheap labor and as early as 1900 the bulk of the employees in all the leading industries was of foreign origin.

American attitudes toward these newcomers were changing. There had been those who opposed unlimited immigration. There were also those who particularly wanted to keep out people who did not easily fit in with the ways of the descendants of British stock. This feeling was, however, dying down until the new immigration brought in people who seemed much stranger than the Irish and the Germans had in previous decades. There had always been a certain amount of anti-Catholic feeling, and this continued with the Italians becoming the main target rather than the Irish. As hundreds of thousands of Jews poured in from Poland and Russia, anti-Jewish prejudice was inflamed. On the Pacific Coast, opposition to Japanese immigration reached a peak of emotion by 1905 and led to the formation of the Asiatic Exclusion League. In San Francisco the board of education ordered segregated schools for Asiatic pupils, even though there were only ninety-three Japanese students in the city.

Even among the well-intentioned, including many of the progressives, there was fear that so many immigrants of such divergent backgrounds could not be assimilated into American life for generations. Some people advocated restriction of immigration so that a small number could be properly "Americanized." This approach implied that the sooner every immigrant dressed, talked and acted in every respect like the Anglo-Saxon ideal, the better off he would be. As yet there was little, if any, respect for the customs and traditions of other lands, and little feeling that these strangers had anything worthwhile to contribute to the cultural life of America. Even those who believed that America was the melting pot into which all foreigners could be put and emerge the better for it, saw the strangers coming out as copies of themselves, not as a new type of citizen.

Those who thought the immigrants could be assimilated were saying, in effect, that environment was more important than heredity. This belief had always been strongly held by those who saw the New World as a place where the human race would build a new and better civilization. There were some, however, who contended that race and heredity were all-important and that the nation was about to degenerate as its genetic inheritance became overwhelmed by what they considered inferior races. This point of view reached its extreme statement in *The Passing of the Great Race* (1916). The author was Madison Grant, himself the perfect example of Anglo-Saxon patrician stock whose ancestors had been prominent in America since Colonial times. In his book he wrote:

> We Americans must realize that the altruistic ideals which have controlled our social development during the past century, and the maudlin sentimentalism that has made America "an asylum for the oppressed," are sweeping the nation toward a racial abyss. If the Melting Pot is allowed to boil without control, and we continue to follow our national motto and deliberately blind ourselves to all "distinctions of race, creed, or color," the type of native American of Colonial descent will become as extinct as the Athenian of the age of Pericles, as the Viking of the days of Rollo.

As the numbers of the immigrants grew larger and their ways more alien to settled Americans, many different attempts were made to control their arrival and to regulate their activities after they landed. Some states required that attorneys be citizens. New York State set the same requirement for private detectives, and Michigan for barbers. More broadly, there were moves to restrict by one means or another the number who could enter the United States. A Federal law in 1902 effectively excluded Chinese laborers and resulted in a boycott of American goods in China. In 1907 President Roosevelt, with the aid of William Howard Taft and Elihu Root, went to great pains to work out an agreement with Japan that would soothe that nation's pride and also keep the extreme anti-Oriental element in California happy. The result was a "gentlemen's agreement" by which the Japanese undertook not to let common laborers emigrate to the United States. A frequently proposed device for reducing the flow of immigration was the literacy test. President Cleveland vetoed one such bill in 1897, President Taft vetoed another in 1913 and Wilson refused to approve two such bills, in 1915 and 1917. However, on the last occasion both houses of Congress passed the bill over the presidential veto. By the terms of this law, no alien over sixteen years of age, who could not read English or some other language, would be admitted to the United States.

Meanwhile, these strangers from overseas were coming in on every ship, with New York City the leading port of entry. Ellis Island, in New York Harbor, through which immigrants had to pass before they were admitted, became a symbol of all that the great change meant, both to the newcomers and to the nation. For most immigrants, the new life began with a sea voyage in the worst accommodations offered by the ship lines, although by the twentieth century conditions were far better than they had been before the steamship. Now the Atlantic crossing took ten days or less but conditions were still crowded.

Confused and bewildered by the noise of an American city such as New York, the new arrival sought others of his own kind—those who had arrived earlier from his country or, better yet, from his own province or village. Here, at least, his language could be understood, and advice secured as to how to go about finding a place to live and a job. Nationality groups thus tended to live in distinct areas. In New York the lower East Side has traditionally been the home of new ethnic groups. The Irish and Germans had first settled here, but moved up Manhattan Island as Italians moved into the Irish areas, and Jews into the German neighborhoods. The Germans for the most part went up the east side of Manhattan, the Irish up the west.

The immigrant was soon living in one of New York's dark and noisy tenements. He had not been used to much in the way of living conditions at home, but at least there had been some fresh air. This, however, was the land of opportunity and his next need and desire was for a job. America's continually expanding economy was in his favor, but he had to start at the bottom. There were common-laborer jobs for the men, digging trenches for sewer pipes, or putting down tracks for the expanding urban trolleys and subways. The women and children were likely to do their work at home, sewing and stitching on a piece-work basis. The pay was miserable, but it kept the family together until better jobs could be secured, and while the newcomers became Americans.

The best schools were not in the districts where the immigrants lived, but most parents took pride in getting their children started in the American school system. This speeded up the Americanization of the youngest generation, but, as many people found to their sorrow, it also began separating the younger generation from the older by language and custom.

It was not long, either, before the nation's newest citizens took an interest in politics. The talk of the progressives about municipal reform, antitrust legislation and similar problems was meaningless to the immigrant. He had no experience in self-government. He needed and wanted practical help with personal and family problems, and society and government did not provide that on any worthwhile scale. As a result an alliance quickly grew between the new masses in the cities and the politicians who operated the party machines and thereby controlled the city governments. The boss got a job for the newcomer, secured medical aid for his family, helped him if he got into trouble with the law. In return the newcomer voted as he was told. The immigrants in this way contributed to corruption in municipal government, but they were not responsible for starting it.

Another kind of migration was bringing into the cities large numbers of equally disadvantaged persons, but these people were native-born, American citizens, except for a certain number from the Caribbean area. They were, of course, American Negroes, many of whom belonged to the first generation to be born free. They came mostly from the rural South, where their social and economic status had, on the whole, deteriorated rather than improved in the later years of the nineteenth century. They settled especially in New York, Philadelphia and Chicago.

There had been Negroes in New York City for generations, but at the turn of the century they were not living in any one particular area. In 1900 there were about 60,000 blacks in the city. The number then increased quite rapidly, reaching 90,000 by 1910. As the numbers went up, there was more prejudice and this was a factor in the development of what became the largest Negro ghetto in the world—Harlem in northern Manhattan Island. In the 1880's Harlem had been a fashionable residential section for middle-class and upper-middle-class families. The area was so far uptown that it could be termed New York's first suburb. By 1914, though, 50,000 Negroes lived in the neighborhood. By 1920, 73,000 people, two-thirds of Manhattan's Negro population, had made Harlem synonymous with the urban life of the American black.

Suffering the disadvantages of the European immigrants—such as poverty, lack of education, and unfamiliarity with city life—the Harlem Negro also became the victim of the greedy landlord and the low-paying employer. Nevertheless, Negroes continued to move to the northern cities and to create a culture and a way of life apart from the white world they could not join. A Negro literature began to develop, along with other manifestations of cultural life, although results were not generally visible until the 1920's. The beginnings of a literary renaissance appeared with such books as *The Autobiography of an Ex-Colored Man* (1912) by James Weldon Johnson (1871–1938) and *Songs of Jamaica* (1912) by Claude McKay (1890–1948).

Change was the order of the day in America. And each change had both a cause and an effect. The cities grew as men and women from farms and foreign countries moved into them. As the cities grew, they began to overshadow the small towns and farming areas in setting the tone and pace of American life. The new kind of city required, for example, new means of transportation and communication, and when these were developed they changed the way people lived. America altered, in some way, all immigrants who came to its shores, but the customs and traditions they brought with them had their effects on the native-born population. These many interacting forces, resulting chiefly from urban growth and immigration, probably did more than anything else to make twentieth-century America a new and different nation.

6 *Theodore Roosevelt Abroad*

AROUND THE WORLD the twentieth century opened with imperialism rampant and the great powers involved in dangerous rivalries. The day of colonization, however, was about over. Imperialism now took the form of domination of foreign lands and their people for economic purposes—to create trading areas for one's own nation and to keep competing nations out.

At this game Great Britain was still the leader. Queen Victoria, the queen-empress who personified Great Britain's empire on which the sun never set, died in 1901. King Edward VII carried on the tradition as Britain began to take sides in the competition among the other powers. Germany, under William II, was becoming a threat to British supremacy both industrially and as a naval power. With Edward's assistance, Great Britain reached an understanding with her old enemy France in 1904, and in 1907 signed an agreement with Russia, with whom France was allied. Arrayed against this group was the already existing Triple Alliance of Germany, Austria-Hungary and Italy. In the Far East, Japan and Russia were on the verge of conflict as they both sought a larger share of the trade of China. The European powers, along with Japan which was rapidly adopting Western industrialism, dominated the world, but they found the world growing smaller as their interests conflicted in the remaining lucrative areas for economic expansion.

Into this situation there entered rather abruptly a new factor: the United States of America. This was partly the result of America's growing population, very much the result of its recently achieved first place in the world industrially, and most immediately the result of its Spanish-American War conquests. These achievements had awed the other nations and had forced America to become involved in world affairs whether she wanted to or not. There was, though, a large and vocal portion of the American people who did not want anything to do with imperialism. They were led by William Jennings Bryan, whose popular following had declined from the peak of enthusiasm it had reached in 1896 when he was the Democratic candidate for president.

On the other side was an equally strong and vocal segment which called for the United States to take its place alongside the great powers of Europe and Asia. There was never a clear-cut vote that gave the people a chance to decide the issue once and for all, but the imperialists carried the day, led as they were by those who controlled the nation's business and government. The spirit of the new imperialists, much like that which extended the nation across the American continent, was expressed by Senator Albert J. Beveridge of Indiana in 1900:

> Our largest trade henceforth must be with Asia. The Pacific is our ocean. . . . The power that rules the Pacific . . . is the power that rules the world. And, with the Philippines, that power is and will forever be the American Republic. . . . God has not been preparing the English-speaking and Teutonic peoples for a thousand years for nothing but vain and idle self-contemplation and self-admiration. No! He has made us the master organizers of the world to establish system where chaos reigns.

At this point fate and the American people chose Theodore Roosevelt to be the chief executive, and he was not at all averse to leading the nation onto the world stage. He was also, if that was the path to be followed, as good a choice as the nation could have made. By background and education and by his personal familiarity with foreign countries, Roosevelt was well prepared for leadership, and he moved in a circle of like-minded men, many of them of considerable ability. He was aware of the growing interdependence of the world and he believed the United States must be involved in that world. He particularly recognized the importance of the Far East in the years ahead. While he was conscious of the war danger posed by the rivalries of the strong nations, he thought armed conflict could be avoided. Because there was this danger, and because he wanted America involved in world affairs, Roosevelt was an advocate of a powerful American Navy. His favorite adage expressed his views on how a nation should act: "Speak softly and carry a big stick." He judged nations and the world in moral terms. To him some wars were "just" and some were "unjust." He had as his chief aides men with the same outlook on the world: William Howard Taft, who served him in various capacities, and John Hay (1838–1905) and Elihu Root (1845–1937), both of whom served as secretary of state.

Even before Roosevelt became president, the United States was caught up in an unusual incident in the Far East which involved military cooperation with other powers. A Chinese secret society, the Boxers, whose purpose was to drive all foreigners out of China, began an uprising in 1900 that by June had several hundred Europeans and Americans surrounded and besieged in Peking. The siege was not lifted until August, when an international force of troops from Great Britain, France, Russia, Germany, Japan and the United States fought its way from Tientsin to rescue the diplomats, businessmen, missionaries and their families. The powers forced China to pay an indemnity of $333,000,000. The United States eventually used a good part of its share for scholarships for Chinese students in the United States.

The year before the Boxer Rebellion Secretary of State Hay had asked all the powers to respect Chinese sovereignty and to allow other nations to trade in their respective spheres of influence. Although the powers expressed agreement only in vague terms, Hay, in March, 1900, declared that his "Open Door" policy had been accepted since no one had actually rejected the idea. While it was intended to prevent the disappearance of China as an independent nation, the Open Door would also make it possible for the United States to trade in all parts of China without having to take over and dominate by force any particular part of China.

Nearer home, the United States was still closely concerned in Cuban affairs. When that newly free nation drew up a constitution in 1900, the United States forced it to include a number of provisions that became known as the Platt Amendment, for the American senator who sponsored them in Congress. The result was that Cuba's new constitution gave the United States veto power over her foreign relations, recognized the right of America to intervene to protect life and property, and granted a naval base which was established at Guantanamo Bay.

Until war began in 1914 the Far East occupied the attention of the American people and their leaders as much as did Europe. This came about because of America's new position in the Pacific, resulting from the Spanish-American War, and because the European powers and Japan were active rivals in rich, enormous but powerless China. At the time Roosevelt became president it appeared that Russia might soon be the dominant power in China. Roosevelt deplored the situation when the Russians encroached on Manchuria, but he could do little about it. One result of Russia's moves was the Anglo-Japanese alliance of 1902.

This rivalry in the Far East came to a head in 1904, when Japan and Russia went to war because of their conflict over spheres of influence in Manchuria and Korea. The war began in February with a surprise attack by the Japanese, without a declaration of war, on Port

Arthur where they bottled up the Russian fleet. They captured the port and destroyed the Far Eastern part of the Russian Navy. In land fighting they pushed the Russians north in Manchuria. In May, 1905, the Japanese Navy annihilated an ineffectual Russian fleet that had sailed all the way from the Baltic Sea.

By now both sides were ready to negotiate peace as neither was in a military or financial condition to carry on the war much longer. Acting on a secret request from Japan, President Roosevelt arranged a peace conference at Portsmouth, New Hampshire, in August, 1905. By the terms of a treaty worked out there, Russia acknowledged the paramount interest of Japan in Korea and made other concessions. Both nations agreed to restore Manchuria to China. Neither side got any indemnity from the other, although the Japanese tried hard to insist on one. The war had some far-reaching results. Russia's threat to China was destroyed and unrest stemming from the disastrous war helped to trigger the Russian Revolution of 1905, which forced the Czar to establish, at least on paper, a constitutional monarchy. Japan, which had been favored by most Americans when the war began, emerged as a world power and soon was felt to be a rising menace to the United States in the Pacific. The balance of power in the Far East was destroyed. President Roosevelt, who greatly enjoyed his role as peacemaker between two great powers, found his reputation enhanced around the world and the next year he received the Nobel Prize for Peace for his efforts.

This active president was also eager to play a role in European affairs and to deal as an equal with the heads of the nations there. He believed that America should participate in international affairs in order to help maintain peace and the dominance of Western European civilization. In particular Roosevelt sought better relations with Great Britain. The old animosity and suspicion that had been born of the American Revolution and the War of 1812 were slow in disappearing, but for some years relations had improved. Roosevelt thought that the two English-speaking nations had much in common and should be friends.

An opportunity for Roosevelt to play a leading role in European affairs came in 1905–06 when trouble arose over Morocco. The French—with the passive acceptance of other nations, especially Spain and Great Britain—had for some time been taking steps that would make France the dominant power in this North African area. Germany, anxious to catch up with France and England as an imperial power in Africa and elsewhere, challenged the French action. A speech by the German Emperor in Tangiers in March, 1905, with a demand for an international conference over Morocco, came as close to bringing about a European war as any event prior to the actual outbreak nine years later.

William II asked President Roosevelt to intervene, but at first he didn't feel he could or should. As the situation grew worse, Roosevelt changed his mind and, in a complicated series of secret negotiations, persuaded all the parties involved to take part in an international conference, at which the United States would be represented, in January, 1906, in Algeciras, Spain. At the conference the United States took the side of the French and the British on most questions, but at the same time its representatives tried to soothe the German Kaiser. The conference resulted in a diplomatic triumph for France. It also resulted in some criticism in the United States on the grounds that the country should not "meddle" in European affairs. In effect, Roosevelt had declared that American interests were directly affected by what went on in Europe, and his actions in the Far East had had similar implications for that area.

Roosevelt also had the United States play an active part at the Second International Peace Conference at The Hague, in 1907. Nothing practical concerning disarmament or the limitation of methods of warfare came of the conference, and a court of international justice proposed by the United States was voted down.

In the Western Hemisphere, President Roosevelt also played an active role. To the north of the United States there was one controversy with Canada early in the century. There had been some argument over the southern boundary of Alaska with Canada, but no one had cared until the discovery of gold in the Klondike in 1896 made the question of access to the area of considerable practical importance. Roosevelt blustered about it quite a bit but finally agreed to a treaty which provided for six jurists to decide the location of the disputed boundary. The three Americans the President chose were hardly impartial and, in effect, were ordered by him to support the American position. On the other side were two Canadians and one Briton. The Briton voted for the most part on the side of the United States, and so the matter was settled. On the whole the American position seemed justified, but Roosevelt's attitude and actions were more belligerent than necessary.

More serious difficulties arose to the south, in Latin America. The United States still held firmly to the Monroe Doctrine, as set forth by President James Monroe in 1823, which said that this country would not allow any foreign power to acquire territory in the Western Hemisphere. Sometimes, however, a European nation had a legitimate complaint against a Latin American country, but found it difficult to get satisfaction by peaceful methods. In late 1902, for example, Great Britain, Germany and Italy were unable to collect debts owed them by the dictator of Venezuela, Cipriano Castro. The three nations sent naval ships, blockaded five Venezuelan ports and bombarded some forts. They denied any intention to take over territory, but Germany's actions—in particular the bombarding of a fort and a neighboring village while an arbitration conference was going on in Washington—aroused American opinion. Eventually the dispute was settled by arbitration.

The Venezuelan affair and other incidents, combined with the United States' increased interest in Latin America resulting from the acquisition in 1903 of the area through which the Panama Canal was to be built, caused President Roosevelt to announce in 1904 the Roosevelt Corollary to the Monroe Doctrine. No one, he said, should interfere in the affairs of a Latin American nation as long as those affairs were conducted decently and properly. However, he continued, "brutal wrongdoing, or an impotence which results in a general loosening of the ties of civilized society, may finally require intervention by some civilized nation, and in the western hemisphere the United States cannot ignore this duty." In other words, the Monroe Doctrine was extended so that while it denied European nations the right to intervene, it sanctioned such action when carried out by the United States.

In the course of the Roosevelt and Taft administrations, the United States did intervene in the Caribbean and in South and Central America numerous times. In the Caribbean area, the nation's interests were primarily a matter of national defense because of the nearness of some of the islands to the American mainland and to the Panama Canal which was under construction for ten years beginning in 1904. In other areas, America's primary interest was economic because of growing investments of American capital, particularly in Mexico.

The Roosevelt Corollary was first applied in Santo Domingo. That nation's financial situation was desperate, and it asked Roosevelt to intervene to protect it from its European creditors. The President obliged in 1905 and in about two years American administration of its finances made it solvent again. Such intervention, though, often led to involvement in the domestic and foreign affairs of a nation. In 1912 President Taft forced the Dominican President to resign; in 1916 American Marines landed and, in effect, ruled the land for some years. About this same time the Marines also landed in Haiti and Nicaragua, so that for a good deal of the period these nations were American protectorates on one pretext or another. The

President of Cuba in 1906 asked for American intervention and Roosevelt sent Taft, then secretary of war. When order was restored, the United States withdrew. These continuous military and financial interventions, as well-intended as they were and as much good as they did in some respects, did not endear the United States to its weaker southern neighbors. Secretary of State Elihu Root did his best to act the good neighbor at this time. He established personal relations with Latin American ambassadors and was a co-sponsor of the Central American Peace Conference of 1907. An extended tour he made of Latin America in 1906 was an effective gesture.

Roosevelt, who always had a special place in his patriotic emotions for the United States Navy, recognized its importance with respect to the nation as a world power and, nearer home, for hemispheric defense. Back in 1880 the American Navy had ranked twelfth among the navies of the world. By the start of the century it was third, with seventeen battleships and six armored cruisers. Roosevelt in his very first message to Congress as president made proposals for strengthening the Navy, and kept after the subject all the time he was in office. At the end of his second term the Navy was, in fighting terms, twice as strong as in 1900.

In 1907 Roosevelt resolved on a dramatic display of American naval strength: the fleet would sail around the world. There was considerable opposition at home, because of the cost and also on the grounds that it might cause the Japanese to attack the fleet without notice. Roosevelt persevered and on December 16, 1907, sixteen modern battleships, which because of their light color became known as "The Great White Fleet," steamed out of Hampton Roads, Virginia. The 14,000 men on the ships were under the command of Rear Admiral Robley D. Evans who saluted his commander in chief as the one-time Rough Rider stood proudly on the bridge of the presidential yacht *Mayflower*. Contrary to some expectations, the fleet and the sailors received an enthusiastic welcome in Japan, as they did at other ports of call in Australia, New Zealand and at Gibraltar. On February 22, 1909, the fleet returned home. It was greeted by an exuberant President Roosevelt, who in a matter of days would cease to be president and commander in chief, but who would not cease to speak his mind on America's place in the world.

7 *William Howard Taft at Home*

WHEN THE TIME FOR the presidential election of 1908 approached, Theodore Roosevelt had to make one of the most important decisions of his career. Should he run for reelection? Immediately after his triumph in 1904 he had said he would not seek another term, but his many enthusiastic supporters would overlook this if he changed his mind. There was no doubt that he could have the Republican nomination again in 1908 if he wished it, and little doubt that he would be reelected. Roosevelt did not change his mind. Although only fifty years old and as energetic as ever, he did not feel he could break the third-term tradition, even though he had been elected only once.

If he would not run, he could and did pick his successor. When the Republican convention met it was clear that Roosevelt wanted his close friend and trusted aide, William Howard Taft, nominated. The Republicans named Taft on the first ballot. The Democrats chose William Jennings Bryan for a third time, but the orator from the West no longer aroused the enthusiasm he had a dozen years before. Bryan claimed he was a more worthy successor to Roosevelt because his views were more progressive than those of Taft, but the voters chose Taft. Taft received 321 electoral votes to Bryan's 162 after a dull campaign, but Taft's margin in the popular vote was only half that of Roosevelt's four years before.

The new chief executive who took office in March, 1909, was a completely different personality from his predecessor, although they were very good friends. Where Roosevelt was lively to the point of restlessness, Taft was quiet and easygoing. Roosevelt liked to be boss and he enjoyed the tumult and shouting of political campaigns. Taft was a good administrator and much more at home in a judicial atmosphere than in politics. The two men were unlike physically, also. Taft, although under six feet tall, weighed about 350 pounds and there were many jokes about his size, none of which bothered the genial Taft. He was also the first president to play golf.

William Howard Taft (1857–1930) was born in Cincinnati, Ohio, into a prominent local family. He went to Yale University and became a lawyer. His national career began in 1890 when President Benjamin Harrison appointed him solicitor general. It was then that he became acquainted with Roosevelt, which later led to his first important assignment in the Philippines. During Roosevelt's second term Taft was secretary of war, but Roosevelt used him as his personal envoy on various kinds of missions and Taft often spoke for the President.

As soon as his friend was sworn in, Roosevelt sailed on a much-publicized big-game safari to Africa. A newspaper cartoon showed the animals of Africa fleeing in panic at the news the Rough Rider was coming. His accounts of the trip, for which he received $50,000, appeared in *Scribner's Magazine*. Almost a year later the ex-president's expedition ended with a trip down the Nile. Then came a triumphant tour of Europe, during which he met most of the monarchs of the day. On horseback beside the German Kaiser, he reviewed that ruler's troops; he was invited to lecture at the Sorbonne in Paris and at Oxford University in England. King Edward VII died in May, 1910, while Roosevelt was still in Europe, and Taft asked him to represent the United States at the funeral. He did this with great enthusiasm, and in civilian dress outshone the uniformed kings and princes, although he would have been happier if he could have worn his old uniform as colonel of the Rough Riders. For Roosevelt, the dream of every American boy had come true: cowboy, war hero, nation's leader, big-game hunter, world figure.

Meanwhile, back in Washington, President Taft was having a difficult time. He intended to carry out his predecessor's program, but he was not much of a progressive at heart and he was caught between the conservatives and the progressives in his own party. The latter were becoming increasingly influential in Congress, which now included younger and more liberal men in both parties. The first break between the new president and the progressives occurred because he backed the regular Republicans in their support of the reactionary, domineering Speaker of the House of Representatives, Joseph G. Cannon, when the insurgents attempted to curb his power.

The most important issue facing the new president was that of tariff revision. Unlike the leadership of the Republican Party, Taft was in favor of lower tariffs and had pledged himself if elected to call a special session of Congress to lower tariff rates. This he did in 1909 and a bill carrying some substantial reductions went through the House of Representatives without much difficulty. In the Senate, however, it was different. There, under the leadership of one of the foremost high-tariff advocates of all time, Senator Nelson Aldrich, the original bill was amended and amended. The final Payne-Aldrich bill, a compromise between the House and the Senate, did include substantial reductions in rates on some goods, but on the whole it made little change in the general amount of protection given American products. As innovations, the law established a tariff commission and imposed a small income tax on corporations engaged in interstate commerce.

Taft signed the new tariff bill somewhat reluctantly, but in the fall of 1909 he went on a speaking trip in which he defended it in one speech as the best tariff act ever passed. This was the final blow to the midwestern progressives. They decided that Taft had been converted to the high tariff views of the eastern wing of the Republican Party which represented the industrial interests at the expense of the farmers.

Taft's inept handling of a controversy over conservation also drove him and the progressives further apart. Gifford Pinchot, chief forester and a favorite of Roosevelt, accused Taft's secretary of the interior, Richard A. Ballinger, of handling the leasing of some government-owned coal land in Alaska in a corrupt manner. The progressives seized on this as a further way to get at Taft. Muckraking articles in a number of magazines helped build up public excitement. When, in early 1910, the excitable Pinchot wrote a letter full of unproven accusations to Senator Jonathan P. Dolliver, Taft had no choice but to dismiss him. The anti-Taft elements in Congress then forced an investigation which, however, exonerated Ballinger. But public opinion had already turned against the secretary of the interior and in 1911 he resigned.

One of the most ominous results of the affair was that it put Taft and Roosevelt on opposite sides of a public issue and made Taft appear to be against the conservation policies of his predecessor. Actually Taft did as much for the conservation of natural resources as Roosevelt, although he did not get credit because he did not publicize himself and his actions as well. Taft was the first president to set aside Federal lands where oil had been discovered for future use in the public interest and he also got from Congress the power to reserve coal lands and to set up a bureau of mines.

Taft also suffered an embarrassing setback in foreign affairs when he tried to negotiate with Canada a reciprocity treaty that would reduce the tariff barriers between the two countries. Canada was an exporter of agricultural products and other raw materials, while she imported almost all the manufactured goods she needed. Early in 1911 the United States and Canada negotiated a treaty that ended altogether any tariff between the two nations on most agricultural goods and on many manufactured items. The eastern industrialists at first favored the treaty, although some later turned against it for fear it would set a precedent of lower tariffs. The farmers, whose leaders in Congress were the midwestern progressives, were entirely opposed. Taft took pleasure in pointing out that this showed the progressives were not in principle in favor of low tariffs but were really just as selfish about their own local interests as were businessmen. In the House the reciprocity bill passed because the Democrats supported it. The Senate did not act, so Taft stubbornly called a special session which further alienated him from his own party. Both houses of Congress then passed the bill, but to Taft's chagrin and disappointment, the Canadian government refused to approve the plan.

In foreign affairs in general, Taft was less active—and sounded less aggressive—than Roosevelt. He believed his administration should use diplomatic methods to expand American business abroad. As he expressed it in his last message to Congress in December, 1912:

> This policy has been characterized as substituting dollars for bullets. It is one that appeals alike to idealistic, humanitarian sentiments, to the dictates of sound policy and strategy, and to legitimate commercial aims.

This "dollar diplomacy" was almost as effective in extending American influence over weaker nations as was armed intervention.

There were a number of solid but unspectacular achievements of Taft's rather unhappy administration, some of which were to have long range effects. In 1912 New Mexico and Arizona were admitted to the union as the forty-seventh and forty-eighth states, and it was to be nearly half a century before any more were added. The Interstate Commerce Commission was strengthened. In the Post Office Department a postal savings system—in effect, a savings bank for persons with low incomes—was established and parcel post added for the convenience of all Americans. Most important for the future were two proposed amendments to the Constitution, although neither was finally ratified until 1913. The Sixteenth Amendment gave Congress the power to levy taxes on the incomes of individuals, while the Seventeenth took the power of electing United States senators away from the state legislatures and gave it to the voters themselves.

The most significant event of Taft's presidency, though, was the rift that developed between the two old friends, the ex-president and his successor. Apparently Roosevelt was first made unhappy when Taft replaced some of the former's cabinet appointees with men of his own choosing. Roosevelt thought he had promised he would retain them. While the big-game hunter was on his safari and after he emerged to visit Europe, the progressives began to bombard him with complaints about Taft for, in their eyes, deserting the cause. The Pinchot-Ballinger affair did more than anything else to break up the old friendship, especially when the embittered Pinchot rushed off to Egypt to tell his troubles to Roosevelt. Roosevelt had said he was staying out of politics for a while, but as soon as he arrived back in the United States in June, 1910, he began seeing a steady stream of politicians at his home in Oyster Bay, Long Island. They were almost all from the progressive, anti-Taft wing of the Republican Party.

At the practical, political level, Roosevelt felt Taft was responsible for the decline of the popularity of the Republican Party and the bickering that was splitting it. Everyone was predicting a Democratic triumph in November, and the prediction came true. The Democrats won control of the House of Representatives in 1910 for the first time since 1892 by a margin of 228 to 161. In the Senate the Republicans lost ground but still retained control, at least officially. However, the small group of progressive Republican senators held the balance of power, which made the result all the more bitter for the regulars. In general, western progressives won while eastern regulars lost. The second half of Taft's term was thus doomed to be even more uncomfortable for him than the first. Republican prospects for the 1912 presidential election were depressing indeed, with the rising Democratic tide and the presence on the political scene once more of Theodore Roosevelt, this time as the leader of the anti-administration forces within the party.

8 *Woodrow Wilson and Reform*

As the dates for the nominating conventions for the 1912 presidential race drew near, the fight within the Republican Party grew in intensity, and the split between the progressives and the regulars became complete. For a time, Senator Robert M. LaFollette was the leading contender for the progressives, but many Republicans were waiting to see what Roosevelt would do. When he announced in February, 1912, that he was a candidate for the nomination, the contest developed into a bitter name-calling battle between the one-time friends, Taft and Roosevelt.

The Republicans met in Chicago in June and it soon became apparent that the Taft conservatives controlled the party machinery. Roosevelt led his followers out of the convention and called for the founding of a new party at a convention in August. Here Roosevelt became the candidate of the Progressive Party amid scenes of fervent enthusiasm. "We stand at Armageddon, and we battle for the Lord," Roosevelt declaimed, and when he said, "I am feeling like a bull moose," that animal became the symbol of the new party. Roosevelt split the Republican Party, and by leaving it turned it over to the conservatives. The Progressives' platform called for national regulation of big business and for social welfare legislation of many kinds.

The Democrats convened in June, after the Republican Party meeting but before the Progressives assembled. It was already clear that the Republicans were tearing themselves apart and so the Democratic nomination was a prize eagerly sought. The two leading contenders were Champ Clark (1850–1921) of Missouri, Speaker of the House of Representatives, and Woodrow Wilson (1856–1924), Governor of New Jersey. At the start Clark had more votes than Wilson, but not enough for the nomination because the Democrats required a two-thirds vote. When William Jennings Bryan and others threw their support to Wilson, he finally won the nomination on the forty-sixth ballot.

The three-cornered political campaign that followed was mostly a contest between Roosevelt and Wilson. The mood of the country called for reform, and the question was whether Roosevelt's or Wilson's path was the better to follow in that quest. These two also had great personal drawing power, while Taft seemed dull and uninspiring by comparison with the fervor of his competitors.

Roosevelt stood for the Square Deal, a phrase he used frequently, and for the New Nationalism, a term he had picked up from *The Promise of American Life,* a book published in 1909. The author was Herbert Croly (1869–1930), an editor and reformer, whose book had considerable influence on Roosevelt, at least in helping him express his ideas for solving the nation's problems. The most pressing issue still was how to deal with the trusts and their monopolistic tendencies. Roosevelt believed that large business combinations were here to stay, and that it was either impossible or useless to try to break them up into smaller units. He advocated strict government regulation of large combinations instead. The ex-president campaigned strenuously as usual. In October, in Milwaukee, he was shot in the chest as he left his hotel for the hall where he was to speak. He insisted on speaking, without knowing whether or not the wound was serious. It turned out on examination that no great damage had been done, but once more Roosevelt was a hero.

On first seeing and hearing Wilson in action, people might think he was cold and remote, but his fervor for reform quickly began to communicate itself through his well-phrased rhetoric. He built up a national following eager to let him lead them along the path he proclaimed as the best route to more economic justice for everyone. Wilson's program became known as the New Freedom. In the campaign he differed with Roosevelt in two ways. Where the latter would regulate monopoly, Wilson would break up big business and restore competition. Wilson also opposed Roosevelt's social welfare program, such as minimum-wage laws and the regulation of hours of work, as paternalistic and something the Federal government should not undertake. Wilson, by his background, tended toward the Jeffersonian ideal of democracy which avoided the centralization of power as much as possible.

The election resulted in a close popular vote, with no candidate getting a majority. Wilson received 6,286,000 votes; Roosevelt, 4,126,000; and Taft, 3,484,000. Wilson was a minority president as far as the popular vote was concerned. In the Electoral College, however, Wilson won 435 votes, Roosevelt, 88 and Taft, who carried only Vermont and Utah, 8. The Democrats retained control of the House of Representatives by a large margin and won control of the Senate by a few seats.

When Wilson took office in March, 1913, he was the first Democrat elected to the post in twenty years and only the second since the Civil War. Born in Staunton, Virginia, five years before the war started, the son of a Presbyterian clergyman, Wilson could remember the South in the bitter Reconstruction period. After graduating from Princeton University, he studied law, but soon found that practicing it had little appeal. He returned to school, this time to Johns Hopkins University where he took his Ph.D. in political science in 1886. He began to make a reputation as a professor at Princeton. As an author, his *Congressional Government* was a work of originality, his five-volume *History of the American People* less so but more popular.

In 1902 Wilson was elected president of Princeton, and proceeded to put into effect a number of reforms aimed at improving the quality of the curriculum and making university life more democratic. Here his zeal showed to good advantage. Later a dispute over a new graduate school arose between Wilson and a group headed by a strong-minded dean, and his inability to compromise when he felt he was right became apparent. Wilson resigned the presidency of Princeton in 1910 and that same year was nominated by the Democrats as their candidate for the governorship of New Jersey. Although he was selected by the machine politicians who thought of him as a conservative, he broke with them soon after his election, and forced through the legislature a number of measures that were in keeping with the progressive spirit of the time. His career at Princeton, his switch to politics and his success in that field made him, in a space of two years, a leading prospect for his party's national nomination.

Wilson began his vigorous presidency with some innovations. Instead of sending written messages to Congress, he addressed the two houses in person, something no president since John Adams had done. Believing, as did the Democratic Party in general, in low tariffs, he called Congress into special session to deal with the matter. Between April and October, 1913, the Underwood Tariff Act, named for Representative Oscar W. Underwood, was debated and amended. When finally passed and approved by the President, it was not a free-trade measure but it did, for the first time in more than fifty years, make substantial reductions in import duties. On the average it reduced rates by about 10 per cent. It put wool, iron ore, steel rails, cement, wood pulp and many agricultural products on the free list. The bill also contained the first graduated tax on individual incomes under the recently proclaimed Sixteenth Amendment. This tax was intended to offset the loss in import duties that would result from the Underwood Tariff. For many years these duties had been the largest single source of revenue for the Federal government. The graduated income tax rates ran from one per cent on incomes over $4,000 to six per cent on the highest incomes.

Wilson had also promised reform of the nation's banking system, and he started to carry out the promise at the same time the tariff was being revised. The bankers wanted a strong centralized system controlled by private commercial interests. At the other extreme, the agrarian groups, those who had followed Bryan in his campaigns for "free silver" and cheaper credit, wanted a banking system controlled by the Federal government that would give easy credit. After debates that took up nearly the whole year, Wilson was able to sign, just before Christmas in 1913, the act of Congress which established the Federal Reserve System and finally gave the United States a central banking apparatus that could help control booms and panics.

Under the new law, a central Federal Reserve Board was established as coordinator, with a dozen regional banks in different sections of the country. All national banks had to join the system, and state banks could if they wished. In effect, the member banks owned the reserve banks. The system could issue currency with the full obligation of the government behind it, and could also control the volume of credit by raising or lowering the discount rates it charged member banks. The general result was to provide greater elasticity in expanding or contracting the amount of credit available, to control the amount of money in circulation, and to make it impossible for a few powerful speculators to upset the economy of the country. While neither the bankers nor the more radical reformers were entirely satisfied, the Federal Reserve System proved a success.

A further concession was made to the farm interests in 1916 with the passage of the Federal Farm Loan Act. It created a Federal Farm Loan Board and twelve regional banks, somewhat like the Federal Reserve System. These banks could extend loans on farmlands and buildings through cooperative farm-loan associations. Long-term loans were available and interest rates were moderate. The farm interests claimed they needed such a system because they could not get reasonable terms from commercial banks.

As already noted, Wilson also saw the Clayton Antitrust bill become law and the Federal Trade Commission established in his first term, but otherwise he was more conservative than some of his supporters thought he should be. Although he had not particularly sought it, he signed into law the LaFollette Seamen's Act of 1915 which improved the living and working conditions of men in the merchant marine. A major controversy in Wilson's first term arose when he appointed Louis D. Brandeis (1856–1941) to the Supreme Court in 1916. Brandeis had won a reputation for defending the public against big business by his investigation of insurance practices in Massachusetts, and by his legal arguments for laws setting minimum wages for women. His book *Other People's Money* (1914), critical of the Money Trust, had created a stir and he had been one of Wilson's closest advisors in formulating antitrust legislation. His appointment to the highest court was loudly denounced by the interests he had attacked, but the Senate confirmed him in the post and he served for many years as a distinguished jurist with liberal leanings.

In his relations with Latin America, Wilson was not as successful as he hoped to be. At the start of his administration he announced his good intentions toward Central and South America, yet on the whole he found himself continuing the policies of his predecessors, which had been denounced as imperialistic. Haiti, Santo Domingo and Nicaragua were all occupied by American forces while Wilson was president. It was with Mexico, though, that Wilson had the most difficulty; partly because both he and William Jennings Bryan, whom he had felt obliged to appoint secretary of state because of his support, attempted to enforce their views as to how other nations should manage their affairs.

A counterrevolution, supported by landowners and foreign investors, made Victoriana Huerta president of Mexico in February,

1913, shortly before Wilson became president. Wilson refused to recognize the new government, not because it wasn't in control of the government, but because he didn't consider it legal and constitutional. Wilson's stand did not cause Huerta's downfall. About a year later, in February, 1914, Wilson revoked an arms embargo to allow American arms to be supplied to the opposition leader, Venustiano Carranza. In April a minor incident brought the two nations close to war. When some American sailors landed without permission at Tampico, Mexico, they were seized. They were soon returned but the American admiral demanded an apology and a salute to the flag. Looking for an excuse to intervene, Wilson backed up the admiral and ordered American Marines to land at Vera Cruz. There were casualties on both sides and a war between the United States and Mexico seemed certain. Wilson's tactics were now serving merely to unite all the Mexicans against their neighbor to the north.

At this point Argentina, Brazil and Chile offered to mediate and proposed a new constitutional government for Mexico. Huerta was forced out of office by July, and Carranza assumed the presidency. Almost immediately his chief supporter, Francisco Villa, revolted and Wilson, making a major error, decided to back him. Carranza's forces defeated Villa and Wilson had no choice but to recognize the former's government. Villa then turned to irresponsible banditry. Early in 1916 he seized sixteen Americans and murdered them. About two months later he raided a small town in New Mexico and killed nineteen more Americans. An American Army force under General John J. Pershing was ordered to pursue Villa's gang into Mexico, which it did with little success. Such a foreign invasion further united the Mexicans against the United States. Once again war was near but early in 1917, with the war in Europe overshadowing all other considerations, the American troops were withdrawn. Wilson had spent nearly four years of well-meaning but futile effort to help Mexico and to be a good neighbor. He had sought to foster democratic government and to support Mexico against foreign and economic domination, but his tactics caused Mexican-American relations to remain in an unsatisfactory state for a number of years.

Wilson had come to the presidency believing that the chief executive of the nation should be a leader and should, with his party in Congress, give the country a positive, active government. Wilson did this in his first term, even though his ventures in foreign affairs were not as successful as his domestic reforms. As he faced the problems of the time, he moved more and more toward Roosevelt's position that the Federal government must take action on matters of economic and social concern because no other part of the government was strong enough to oppose the new forces of business and finance. Wilson was also anxious to win the support of all progressives, many of whom were Republican by original allegiance, but some of his actions had displeased them.

At the midterm election in 1914, with most of his domestic program enacted into law and with war having broken out in Europe a few months earlier, Wilson and the Democrats suffered a surprising defeat. Their majority in the House was reduced to about a third of what it had been, although there was no change in the Senate. Among the Republicans, a number of progressives were replaced by members of the party's conservative wing. The progressive tide seemed to have turned and the nation was becoming more and more concerned with the European war.

9 *Life in the United States*

WHEN QUEEN VICTORIA died in 1901, and was succeeded by her eldest son, the sixty-year-old Prince of Wales who became Edward VII, Great Britain had an intelligent and hard-working king. Edward was also worldly and had a considerable reputation as a lover of the gay social life of the upper classes. He reigned for only ten years, but made enough of an impression, especially on the fashionable world, to have the period which covered the pre-World War I years of the century named for him.

The Edwardian Age, in the United States as well as in Europe, was a period of graceful elegance that was soon to seem even more so by contrast with the horrors of war. Most of its elegance and easy living, however, was confined to the rich and the well-born. For them there were large mansions and many servants. In the United States most of those with wealth to show off had acquired it quite recently, from gold or silver mines, railroads, steel mills, and stock market manipulations. Mansions were erected on New York's Fifth Avenue, palatial summer homes were built in various parts of the country. The flow of the newly rich to New York increased after 1900 and most of those who came wanted to get into "society," which was dominated until her death in 1908 by Mrs. William Astor. If you were invited to "Mrs. Astor's ball," you were in society as one of the "400," but if not, you were out.

Entertainment was on a lavish scale. Dinners for a hundred guests were not uncommon, and such affairs went on and on, with seven or eight courses and a variety of wines. At one dinner it took 3,000 roses to make the centerpiece, while at another the host borrowed nightingales from the zoo to adorn the dining room. Perhaps the most unusual dinner of all was the one C. K. G. Billings gave to celebrate the completion of his new stable, which had cost $200,000. At the affair, given at Sherry's, the guests dined while on horseback. New York City's glittering night life catered to the flashier big spenders, as well as to those whom Mrs. Astor recognized. Rector's on Broadway was the favorite hangout of sporting and theatrical society. Here James Buchanan (Diamond Jim) Brady often had midnight supper. An unusually successful salesman of railroad supplies, Diamond Jim had more than a million dollars worth of jewelry, mostly diamonds, and seemed to wear a great deal of it on every occasion. He was frequently in the company of stage star Lillian Russell, the favorite pin-up girl of the era.

Newport, Rhode Island, was the most fashionable summer resort; but Saratoga, with its health springs and its horse races, attracted a livelier crowd. Many of the rich traveled to their favorite resorts by private railroad car or yacht. Early in the century, James Gordon Bennett, proprietor of the *New York Herald,* bought a yacht that cost $625,000. For those who did not have their own railroad cars, but wanted to travel in luxury, the *Twentieth Century Limited,* beginning in 1902, ran between New York and Chicago on the fastest possible schedule. It was famous for its food as well as its speed, and rivalled Delmonico's and Rector's as a favorite dining spot of the rich.

The newspapers gave great amounts of space to reporting the doings of the society world, even stating the cost of private dinner parties—or at least the rumored cost. Nothing attracted more attention in the papers than accounts of weddings in which American heiresses were married to titled Europeans. A typical one was the marriage of Vivien Gould to Lord Decies of England in 1911. The wedding cake cost $1,000 and had electric lights. The bride's father gave her a diamond coronet to wear at the forthcoming coronation of King George V.

Diamond coronets were out of the reach of most Americans, but middle-class citizens of modest income were able to live decently and in some comfort. If incomes were lower than today, so were prices. A middle-class family could afford to live in a moderate-sized, two-story house. A cook could be employed, around 1900, for $5 a week, a waitress for $3.50.

Less money was spent on appliances and household gadgets because only a few existed, although gradually life was being made easier by more machines. Many kitchens still had coal stoves, but the gas range became available early in the century. Electricity was beginning to take over the lighting of houses, and the electrically operated floor-cleaner was becoming practical. Most town houses had bathtubs and water closets, but the homes of factory workers, farmers and those who lived beyond the reach of water and sewer lines did not include such luxuries. The railroads had refrigerator cars, but most families did not have any fresh fruits or vegetables during the winter months. Home canning in the late summer, which caused a great flurry and sometimes short tempers in hot kitchens, provided a substitute.

As more consumer goods were mass-produced and as the potential market expanded because of a growing population and a higher national income, advertising came to play a great role in convincing people they needed the latest gadgets. There were only fifteen advertising agencies in the country in 1900, and advertising was just beginning to be more than an announcement of goods available, or a plug for a patent medicine. The rapid growth of the automobile industry was a considerable stimulant to advertising. So also was the growth of popular magazines with circulations that made it possible to reach hundreds of thousands of people all over the country with a commercial message. In the twenty years after 1902 the *Saturday Evening Post's* advertising revenue went from less than half a million dollars a year to nearly $29,000,000. Catchy slogans were popular: "A Skin You Love to Touch" (Woodbury Soap); "Watch the Fords Go By"; and "His Master's Voice" (Victrola).

The period saw little change in clothing styles and men, as usual, were the drabber sex. Men's suits were almost universally dark and heavy the year round. In the country in the summer one might wear white flannel or white duck, but there was no such thing as a summer-weight suit. Shirts were worn with detachable collars, often made of celluloid for easier cleaning. Cuffs were stiff and detachable too. For the ordinary office worker, the usual headpiece was a derby, but the banker and the man of affairs wore a silk hat and, quite likely, a frock coat. No middle-class man would think of going without a hat; if a man belonged to the laboring class he wore a cap. Men's bathing suits covered almost as much of the body as did the long winter underwear, and they fitted about as well.

Women's clothing of the period was notable for the amount of it. Skirts came down to the ground and it was only after 1910 that they began to creep up a bit. Even for bicycling, or playing tennis or golf (and many people considered these activities extremely unladylike), skirts were only a few inches off the ground. When women began to drive cars, this influenced fashions, causing skirts to go up slightly. The smallest possible waist was a feminine ideal, achieved by a rigid corset reinforced with whalebones. The final effect for the well-dressed woman was a figure pushed in at the stomach, up at the bosom and out in the rear.

Women's shoes were high and they buttoned, although one hardly saw more than the toes of them. Only a few well-to-do women wore silk stockings; everyone else wore black or white cotton hose. Hats were large and much-decorated. Ostrich plumes were popular and some hats featured stuffed birds. In the early years of the century the shirtwaist was worn almost universally, especially by the working girl. Shirtwaists were cheap and could be worn with different skirts to give more variety to one's wardrobe. The shirtwaist became quite daring in 1907 when it became the "peek-a-boo," so-called because it now had small perforations which were embroidered around their edges. From Paris in 1908 came the sheath gown, which was considered quite daring. This was also the year of the large "Merry Widow" hat and the dotted veil.

As early as 1915 the critic H. L. Mencken used the word "flapper" to describe the modern sophisticated young lady, and he noted that by that time her skirts were up to her ankles. The ideal American girl of the period, though, was the "Gibson Girl," named for her creator, artist Charles Dana Gibson (1867–1944). His drawings of her appeared in popular magazines and were eagerly awaited by both sexes. She was slim, small-waisted, and had a pompadour hairdo. Most of all, she had a cool, aloof beauty that made her seem most attractive and able to handle well her multitude of suitors. She was usually pictured with an ideal young man, created by Gibson somewhat in his own image. This new American male was clean-shaven, with a strong jaw and broad shoulders. Gibson's drawings were not just pretty illustrations, but in many cases made sharp and amusing comments on the social scene.

If women's fashions were slow to change, woman's position in the world was changing more rapidly. This was due in large part to the growth of business and the new technology that provided typewriters and telephones and therefore demanded people to operate the machines and the switchboards. About 20 per cent of all American women over fifteen years of age were employed in 1900, and in ten years another 5 per cent were in shops and offices as the number of jobs increased. Wages were low with stenographers receiving from $6 to $8 a week. In 1914 nearly half the nonprofessional women over sixteen were getting less than $6 a week at a time when economists said $7 was needed for bare subsistence living. A few women were succeeding in more professional and more lucrative work. There was, for example, Miss Elsie de Wolfe, who became America's first woman interior decorator and who also became known as "The Chintz Lady."

Women from the middle-class section of society found more time than before to participate in cultural and civic activities. These women had more labor-saving devices, somewhat fewer children, and more education than their ancestors. The General Federation of Women's Clubs, founded late in the previous century, had a million members by 1912. It had paid increasing attention to social conditions after Mrs. Sarah P. Decker, its new president, announced in 1904: "Ladies, I have an important piece of news for you. Dante is dead. He has been dead for several centuries, and I think it is time that we dropped the study of his inferno and turned attention to our own." A few years later, in 1910, a feminist leader, Rheta Childe Dorr, wrote a book titled *What Eight Million Women Want.*

The moral code of society remained strict, whether applied to personal behavior or to the arts. In the early years of the century, in proper society at least, an unmarried girl had to have a chaperone when she went to a social affair, although the custom was dying. Divorce was frowned upon, but the rate was rising and in 1914 there were 100,000 divorces in a single year. In 1908 it was against the law in New York City for a woman to smoke in public but this was somewhat of a last-ditch defense against a practice that was growing too firmly to be halted. The censors and the moralists were busy on the cultural front, led by Anthony Comstock (1844–1915), who had founded the New York Society for the Suppression of Vice in 1873. In 1912 he attacked a painting of a shyly nude maiden, called "September Morn," and thereby called more attention to the uninspired work of art than it would otherwise ever have known. With the aid of the crusading zeal of John S. Sumner, Comstock's successor, Theodore Dreiser's novel, *The "Genius,"* was effectively banned from the bookstores in 1916.

The turn-of-the-century period had its fads and fashions in furniture and interior decoration, too. The style known as Art Nouveau began in Europe, but had considerable impact in the United States just after 1900. It was richly ornamental and was especially effective in the decorative arts—jewelry and book designing as well as furniture. Its chief American exponent was Louis C. Tiffany (1848–1923). He was noted particularly for his glasswork—lamps, vases and windows. His vases might look like growing flowers; a lamp like a tree, with a shade of many pieces of colored glass.

Mission furniture was popular and was part of the crafts movement. The bulky oak furniture was often set off by Navajo rugs. A family could buy a three-piece "Arts and Crafts Library Suite" for $11.95. The spokesman of the crafts movement was Elbert Hubbard (1856–1915), who affected a flat black hat, a cape and a flowing tie. To thousands of Americans avidly seeking true culture he was the prophet of the generation. His magazine, the *Philistine* ("for Booklovers and Folks who Write, Paint and Dream"), attained a circulation of 225,000. Having made money as a soap salesman, Hubbard was an impressive performer as a speaker and what seemed to be sage remarks tripped off his tongue. He ran the Roycroft Press in Aurora, New York, and printed his messages in books with limp leather bindings.

As usual the American Negro was getting little share of the prosperity or the culture. In the United States by 1900 only 2,500 Negroes had graduated from college. More than half of them had become teachers. In the entire South only 8,000 Negro boys and girls were in high school. Nine out of ten Negroes still lived in the South, and more of them were farmers than anything else. There was a steady drift to the cities from the rural areas, and to the North in general. By 1910 Washington, New York and New Orleans each had nearly 100,000 Negroes in their populations.

Except for a brief period after the Civil War, the Negro had never enjoyed full civil rights, but the so-called Jim Crow laws became even stricter after 1900. At that time Georgia was the only state requiring segregation on streetcars, but ten other states passed such laws by 1907. The first law requiring segregation in parks was passed in Georgia in 1905. In politics, too, state laws made it difficult for the Negro to vote. In 1912 even within the Progressive Party some of its white supporters in the South did their best to keep Negroes out of the delegations to the convention that nominated Roosevelt. When the Democrats came to power in 1913, with a president born in the South and led by southerners in Congress, segregation was put into effect in government offices in the capital where it had not existed before. In Atlanta the postmaster dismissed thirty-five Negroes.

Raw, illegal violence was also practiced on the Negro and it was seldom that anyone was punished for such acts. Lynchings, already an old American custom practiced against horse thieves in the West, became common in the South. In 1900, 115 Negroes were illegally killed by mobs, usually by hanging, and the next year a total of 130 lynchings set a record. Until 1913 there were about 50 lynchings a year, but gradually the number decreased. Nor was it only in the South that mobs took justice into their own hands. Two Negroes were lynched in a race riot in Lincoln's home town of Springfield, Illinois in 1908. It was 1918 before anyone was punished in the South for trying to lynch a Negro.

The two leading spokesmen for the Negroes were Booker T. Washington (1856–1915) and William E. B. Du Bois (1869–1963).

While they both fought for more social and economic justice for the blacks, they differed completely as to how this was to be achieved. Washington believed the Negroes should concentrate on education, especially of a vocational nature. They should make themselves useful and be hard-working. Washington did not press for desegregation and civil rights, believing that these would follow in due course. This policy received wide support from white leaders, and philanthropists gave large amounts of money to further these aims. So far as they were concerned, Washington was the proper spokesman for his race. When, however, in October, 1901, President Roosevelt invited Washington to dine at the White House, the reality of race prejudice was quickly revealed. As soon as news of the event got out, southern editors and politicians denounced Roosevelt in vicious and hysterical terms. Washington's autobiography, *Up from Slavery,* appeared that same year and was much praised and widely read.

Du Bois was younger, more of an intellectual, more in tune with the progressive era than was Washington. He did not believe the Negro could ever achieve economic security or self-respect unless he also had the right to vote and full civil rights. Beginning in 1905 Du Bois and others, both black and white, met annually at Niagara Falls, and out of these meetings came the National Association for the Advancement of Colored People, which began operating in 1910. The NAACP soon became the most influential group working for Negro rights and as time went on Du Bois's approach to the struggle for improving the Negroes' condition won out over Washington's methods. Du Bois's general philosophy was first set forth in *The Souls of Black Folk* (1903).

In the area of religious life there were also differences of opinion as to methods and goals. The fundamentalists, on the one hand, were still waging a battle with science that had begun half a century before with the dispute over the theory of evolution. The modernists, on the

Dixon Public Library Dixon, Illinois

other hand, accepted the necessity of reconciling religious belief with science and were more concerned with the place of the church in modern economic and political life. One aspect of this concern took the form of the Social Gospel. The Social Gospel was a liberal movement within American Protestantism that had begun in the second half of the nineteenth century, and its efforts in the new century were in keeping with the atmosphere of the progressive movement. It put even more stress on economic justice and advocated a living wage for every worker. The best-known leader of the movement was Walter Rauschenbusch (1861–1918), author of an influential statement of its goals and ideals in *Christianity and the Social Crisis* (1907). Many Protestant churches, though, did not seem to have much interest in the poorer classes and among some groups—union leaders for example—there was a feeling that the Protestant churches were for the well-to-do. As labor unions grew, they took away some of the appeal of the Social Gospel movement.

The Roman Catholic Church was growing more rapidly than the Protestant denominations because so many immigrants came from Catholic countries. The Catholic Church seemed closer to the workingman, in spite of its long conservative tradition, if for no other reason than that so many Catholics belonged to the laboring class. In the thirty years from 1890 to 1920 the number of Catholics in the United States increased from 9,000,000 to double that figure. When World War I began there were about 22,000,000 Protestants and 16,000,000 Catholics.

The old-fashioned pulpit-thumping type of Christian evangelism was by no means dead. Its most popular practitioner in these years was William A. (Billy) Sunday (1863–1935), who had been a professional baseball player before turning evangelist in 1896. He was ordained a clergyman in 1903 and in a few years was attracting enormous crowds everywhere he went. Sunday was agile on the platform and slangy in his language, but he preached the kind of Bible fundamentalism many wanted to hear. For example, he said in one sermon:

> You turn up your noses at a revival when the very religion which you love was born in a time of revival. I wonder God don't knock you over. Paul was an evangelist, and whenever Paul was to preach or wherever he went they had to call out the police to protect him. . . .

In medicine and science there were notable advances in the first years of the century. The Rockefeller Institute in New York was founded in 1901, with money supplied by John D. Rockefeller, Sr., and it opened its first laboratory in 1904 to further the cause of medical and related sciences. It soon became an institution with international prestige. A report made in 1910 by Abraham Flexner (1866–1959), after a firsthand investigation of American medical schools, sped up a needed reform of their standards, organization and curriculum. Victory over yellow fever and progress in fighting hookworm also marked the early years. In 1900 a commission headed by Walter Reed (1851–1902), for whom the Army hospital in Washington is named, proved by on-the-spot investigation in Cuba that yellow fever was an infection carried by mosquitoes. Several of the doctors and scientists who took part in the investigation paid with their lives, but thereafter it was possible to prevent yellow fever epidemics. In 1902 a young scientist, Charles W. Stiles (1867–1941), advanced the theory that hookworm disease, marked by general lethargy and especially prevalent in the American South, could be controlled by attacking the hookworm parasite which he had identified. (Newspaper headlines proclaimed that the "germ of laziness" had been discovered.) Stiles became active in a campaign to eradicate the disease and was aided by a $1,000,000 gift from Mr. Rockefeller.

In Europe at this time scientists were doing work which was to lead to the opening up of the field of nuclear physics and, eventually, to the atomic bomb. Max Planck (1858–1947), a German physicist, revolutionized his field in 1900 with a statement of the quantum theory. Five years later, Albert Einstein (1879–1955), another German physicist who later became an American citizen, presented his first paper on the theory of relativity. Then in 1913 Niels Bohr (1885–1962), a Danish physicist, reconciled the quantum theory with his general theory of atomic structure.

Psychiatry and behaviorism, two landmarks in the study of human behavior, caused controversy and became popular fads. Sigmund Freud (1856–1939), born in Austria, had begun to set forth his theories before the beginning of the century, but his first important book on psychoanalysis was not translated into English until 1909. That same year he and a fellow worker, C. G. Jung, were invited to the United States to lecture at Clark University in Massachusetts. This trip brought public recognition to Freud and his studies. It also gave to the literary and intellectual world, and others outside that world, a whole new jargon. Even before World War I it was fashionable in such circles to be psychoanalyzed. A little later, in 1912, an American psychologist, John B. Watson (1878–1958), announced his theory of behaviorism. He sought to explain human behavior almost entirely by the physiological response to stimuli; environment alone was important. His ideas did call for subjecting psychology to the techniques of the laboratory, but not everyone agreed with his seemingly extreme position.

The optimistic and reforming attitudes of the era were noticeable in education, which was much influenced by the respect for science and by the ideas of John Dewey (to be considered in the next chapter). Illiteracy dropped steadily and between 1870 and 1900 the number of college graduates tripled while the population doubled. Between 1890 and 1900 the number of secondary schools nearly doubled while the number of students increased from 297,894 to 630,048. By 1918 every state had a compulsory school attendance law.

In less formal ways, culture, education and fellowship were

available through the great variety of organizations which Americans often seem anxious to form and to join. The Chautauqua, represented by a large tent pitched in some open space in the village for a week in the summer, was going strong. Here one could be inspired by a lecture delivered by a national figure, or entertained by a magician and a troupe of Swiss bell ringers. Rotary International was formed in Chicago in 1905 and by 1910 there were enough such clubs around the country to justify the organization of a national association devoted to fellowship among businessmen and service to their communities. The Boy Scouts of America came into being in 1910 and were followed two years later by their sisters, the Girl Scouts.

It was an active period, in which energetic men and women put a great deal of enthusiasm into all kinds of activities: making money, reforming the world, or having fun.

10 The Literary and Intellectual World

THE TECHNOLOGICAL and social changes in the early twentieth century in Western Europe and the United States were reflected in the literary and intellectual world. There was a revolt against the genteel tradition with which the nineteenth century had been associated. To some writers and thinkers, the problems of the urban and mechanized world brought gloom and pessimism. Others joined in the crusading, reforming spirit of the progressives.

The movement toward realism and freedom in the arts started slowly, but gathered force as the prewar years went along. The younger writers, artists and thinkers of America joined in spirit those of Western Europe in experimenting with ideas, words and colors. They moved to the big cities, especially New York and Chicago, and by about 1912–13 they were firmly entrenched there. Chicago had its artistic Bohemia and in New York Greenwich Village was well established as the center of intellectual and artistic ferment. As W. A. Swanberg describes it in *Dreiser* (Charles Scribner's Sons, 1965):

> The Village teemed with atheists, socialists, cubists, anarchists, violinists, poets, free-thinkers, free-lovers, birth-control advocates and women who bobbed their hair and smoked cigarettes, and, if some were crackpots or phonies, others were sincere enough and some were genuinely creative artists or intellectuals. Most of them were conscious rebels. Indeed, the spirit that created the Village as an entity was precisely the spirit that made Dreiser what he was—revolt

> against mildewed American concepts and proprieties, a yearning for a freer and better life along with great confusion as to how to attain it.

The ruling elders of American literature in 1900 were Mark Twain (1835–1910), William Dean Howells (1837–1920), and Henry James (1843–1916). Twain as novelist and commentator on life, and Howells as novelist, critic and magazine editor, had both done their most important work before the new century, although both continued to write. James, who for many years had made his home in England, wrote some of his best stories and novels, such as *The Wings of the Dove* (1902) and *The Ambassadors* (1903) in the prewar years. All three of these elder generation writers were realists, each in his own way. While not as determinedly devoted to finding their themes and characters in the modern urban environment as the younger men, they did break away from nineteenth-century moral and sentimental styles to offer encouragement and leadership to the next generation.

The writer who came to symbolize the new novelists, and eventually to be awarded highest rank among them, was Theodore Dreiser (1871–1945). Born in Indiana, Dreiser was a journalist in several cities before settling down in New York in 1904. His first novel, *Sister Carrie,* appeared in 1900 and was a great disappointment to him. Most reviewers condemned it, the publisher was not enthusiastic and the public was not ready for a novel in which an unchaste woman ended up with a successful career. In 1911 came *Jennie Gerhardt*—the story of a woman who sacrifices her own interests for her lover—which sold better, but was another disappointment to Dreiser. *The "Genius,"* published in 1915, was a long novel about a gifted artist of weak character, and to some extent it was autobiographical. It might have sold better than any of Dreiser's previous work, but it was suppressed as being indecent because of its frankness about sex. Dreiser and his friends, and others opposed to censorship, carried on a long and vigorous battle to free the book. While the fight at that time did Dreiser little good, it did help break down the power of the censor for the future.

In all his novels, such as the famous *An American Tragedy* (1925), Dreiser took a naturalistic view of the world, seeing no moral laws that were effective and suggesting that the individual, generally helpless against the restraints of society, might as well try to get as much for himself as he could. Dreiser's view of the tragedy of life comes through strongly in his writings, despite his often awkward and clumsy style and his lifelong habit of making his books too long. Somehow, the effect is still that of a most powerful writer.

Jack London (1876–1916) represented in his work the new writers' desire to get away from novels about the polite middle-classes. Born in San Francisco, an adventurer, sailor, and participant in the Klondike gold rush in 1897, London wrote of the people and places he knew, and did so with raw energy. Among his best-known novels are *The Call of the Wild* (1903), about a dog who escapes from civilization in the far north; *The Sea-Wolf* (1904), the story of a ruthless, domineering captain of a sealing ship; and *Martin Eden* (1909), which concerns an author's struggles and is partly autobiographical.

Frank Norris (1870–1902) and Upton Sinclair (1878–1968) joined the novelists' wing of the progressive and muckraking movement. Norris, who was born in Chicago, was a published author in his early twenties. Becoming concerned about social problems, he conceived the idea of a trilogy about wheat, only two volumes of which were completed when he died at thirty-two. The first was *The Octopus* (1901), which deals with wheat growing and the struggle between farmers and railroad owners. The second, *The Pit* (1903), is a story of speculation on the wheat exchange in Chicago, and of what happens to a man who puts all his energy into business.

Upton Sinclair, who in his long life became one of America's most successful and prolific novelists, was known in this period for *The Jungle* (1906), which he wrote after taking part in an investigation of the Chicago stockyards and meat-packing plants. It helped secure passage that same year of the first pure food and drug act. Here is a typical passage:

> It seemed as if every time you met a person from a new department, you heard of new swindles and new crimes. There was, for instance, a Lithuanian who was a cattle butcher for the plant where Marija had worked, which killed meat for canning only; and to hear this man describe the animals which came to his place would have been worth while for a Dante or a Zola. It seemed that they must have agencies all over the country, to hunt out old and crippled and diseased cattle to be canned. There were cattle which had been fed on "whisky-malt," the refuse of the breweries, and had become what the men called "steerly"—which means covered with boils.

Sherwood Anderson (1876–1941), although he belonged to this generation, was a late starter. Born in Ohio, he settled down there after some drifting around, became the manager of a paint factory, then one day gave it up to become a writer. His first novel, *Windy McPherson's Son,* did not appear until 1916. He did not receive wide attention as a writer about American life, which he saw as frustrating and puzzling to the ordinary man, until after the publication of his best-known novel, *Winesburg, Ohio* in 1919.

Edith Wharton (1862–1937) wrote chiefly of upper-class people and her work was considerably influenced by Henry James. Her 1905 novel, *The House of Mirth,* told how New York society expelled a girl who needed to make a brilliant marriage but who defied the conventions of the time. The novelette *Ethan Frome* (1911) is a tragic story and differs from much of her work in dealing with simple people. Willa Cather (1873–1947) was a magazine editor who published short stories and poems, but did not write a novel until 1912. This first novel was followed the next year by her much-praised *O Pioneers!* and in 1918 by *My Ántonia.* Ellen Glasgow (1874–1945) was born in Virginia, a member of an aristocratic southern family, and her writings used her native state as their background. *The Voice of the People* in 1900 was the first of many such novels. Gertrude Stein (1874–1946), who in the 1920's was to become the friend and sponsor of yet another generation of writers, lived in Paris most of the time after 1903. Her early collection of stories, *Three Lives* (1909), was popular, but after that her experiments with language made her "difficult" for the casual reader to comprehend.

While writers such as these received most of the critical attention, and while some of their books found a wide audience, most of the public showed more interest in lighter fiction—historical novels, westerns and romances. Maurice Thompson's *Alice of Old Vincennes,* a story about George Rogers Clark and the Northwest Territory, was a best-seller in 1900, as was Mary Johnston's *To Have and To Hold,* which concerned an English noblewoman and a terribly brave Virginian, and which sold 250,000 copies in five months. That same year Booth Tarkington had his first success with an eighteenth-century costume romance, *Monsieur Beaucaire.* The following year a novel of the American Civil War, and another about an imaginary kingdom vied for popularity. *The Crisis* by Winston Churchill (no relation to the British statesman of the same name) was the war story and sold over a million copies. George Barr McCutcheon's *Graustark,* which had brave Americans coming to the rescue of beautiful and noble heroines in a mythical land, sold 150,000 copies in nine months. Churchill later turned to novels that dealt with ethical conflict in American business and political life. Such a book was *Coniston* (1906).

Among writers of westerns and other adventure stories, Owen Wister, Zane Grey, Harold Bell Wright, Rex Beach and Edgar Rice Burroughs were particularly popular. Wister's *The Virginian,* about an ideal cowboy who courts a Vermont-raised school teacher, was a best seller in 1902. Zane Grey's *Riders of the Purple Sage* (1912) was the most popular of his many western stories. Wright's books were somewhat different. They were set in the great outdoors of the Southwest, but Wright was much concerned with wholesome morality, or "muscular Christianity," as one critic put it. His most successful novel was *The Winning of Barbara Worth* (1911) which sold a million and a half copies over a span of twenty-five years. Rex Beach's favorite setting for his stories was the Klondike, an area with which he was familiar, and a typical novel was *The Spoilers* (1906). *Tarzan of the Apes,* the first of a long series by Burroughs, was published in 1914.

Writing in a more sentimental vein were John Fox, Jr., and Alice Rice. Fox achieved national popularity with *The Little Shepherd of Kingdom Come* (1903), and *The Trail of the Lonesome Pine* (1908), both set primarily in the Kentucky mountains. Mrs. Rice is remembered for *Mrs. Wiggs of the Cabbage Patch* (1901), whose widowed main character never stops believing: "Looks like ever' thing in the world comes right, if we jes' wait long enough."

Among the most popular writers of stories for boys and girls were L. Frank Baum, Kate Douglas Wiggin, Gene Stratton-Porter, and Eleanor Porter. Baum's first Oz book, *The Wonderful Wizard of Oz,* appeared in 1900 and was soon followed by others. Mrs. Wiggin's story of a rather precocious little girl, *Rebecca of Sunnybrook Farm* (1903) became famous, as did *Mother Carey's Chickens* (1911), about a warm-hearted widow with a number of children. Mrs. Stratton-Porter's *Freckles* (1904), the story of a boy who thinks he is an orphan but isn't, and *A Girl of the Limberlost* (1909), about a girl who gets money for her education by the unlikely means of catching moths in a swamp and selling them, were highly successful. Equally popular was Pollyana, the "glad child," and heroine of Eleanor Porter's books.

Poetry changed and entered a fresh era of excellence, although it showed results somewhat later than fiction. Signifying the change was *Poetry: A Magazine of Verse,* founded in 1912 by Harriet Monroe

(1860–1936), herself a poet and essayist. Earlier, other new poets had begun to see their work in print. Edwin Arlington Robinson (1869–1935) had been published before the turn of the century and had already caught the attention of Theodore Roosevelt. When *Captain Craig* appeared in 1902 the President appointed Robinson to a quiet clerkship in the Custom House in New York, so that the steady salary could enable him to devote himself to poetry. William Vaughan Moody (1869–1910) had his first verse play, *The Masque of Judgment,* published in 1900; while Sara Teasdale (1884–1933), writing in a quieter, more personal mood, had her *Sonnets to Duse and Other Poems* issued in 1907. Three more volumes followed by 1917. William Carlos Williams (1883–1963) began his long career in 1909 with *Poems.* The even longer poetic career of Ezra Pound (1885–) started that same year with the publication of two volumes of verse, *Personae* and *Exultations.* He was already living in Italy where he has made his home most of his life, and he became a leader of the Imagists. This movement in England and the United States flourished from this time until 1917. It opposed the romantic conception of poetry and advocated the use of common speech, new rhythms and complete freedom in the choice of subject matter.

Pound, who did a great deal as critic and encourager of modern literature and of many writers of the twentieth century, soon lost interest in Imagism. Amy Lowell (1874–1925) then became its moving force, about 1913. The year before, her first book, *A Dome of Many-Coloured Glass,* appeared. Four more volumes of her verse were issued before 1920. Both Robert Frost (1874–1963) and Vachel Lindsay (1878–1931), two poets who found large audiences, were initially published in 1913. Frost was represented by *A Boy's Will,* which was soon followed by other volumes that contained some of his best-known poems, such as "Mending Wall," and "The Road Not Taken." Lindsay's first collection, *General William Booth Enters into Heaven and Other Poems,* was followed the next year by *The*

Congo and Other Poems. He was soon in demand as a reader of his own poems, whose vigorous booming rhythms he declaimed with gusto.

In 1914 another poet soon to reach a popular audience had some of his shorter pieces published in *Poetry.* He was Carl Sandburg (1878–1967) and the poems included "Chicago," which so well captured the spirit of that raw, bustling city. Another of his best-known poems, "Fog," appeared in a volume of his poetry in 1916. Edgar Lee Masters (1868–1950) had been published before 1915 but in that year his *Spoon River Anthology,* verses like epitaphs that revealed the secret lives of those buried in a midwestern cemetery, brought him fame. T. S. Eliot (1888–1965), who achieved the highest critical stature of all, first appeared as a poet in book form in 1917 with *Prufrock and Other Observations.* Born in Missouri, Eliot lived most of his adult life in England and became a British subject.

Meanwhile a revolution in magazine publishing which had begun in the late nineteenth century continued. Technological improvements in papermaking, in printing equipment and in photoengraving made magazines more attractive and aided in the mass production of them. Increased advertising revenue was also helpful. It was in this new kind of magazine that most of the articles of the muckrakers appeared. At the same time there also existed the more intellectual and somewhat old-fashioned kind of literary magazine such as *Century* and *Scribner's.* It was an especially good era for journals of opinion devoted chiefly to public affairs. The *Nation* had been founded shortly after the Civil War; the *Outlook* had its most successful period in the prewar years, with Theodore Roosevelt as a contributing editor after he left the presidency. It serialized Booker T. Washington's autobiography, *Up from Slavery. World's Work* was established in 1900, to publish articles about the "activities of the newly organized world, its problems and even its romances." Walter Hines Page was editor until he was appointed ambassador to Great

Britain in 1913. In 1909 the *Progressive* was established to present the political viewpoint of Robert M. LaFollette and his followers. The *New Republic,* founded in 1914, was the magazine most representative of the era of the New Nationalism and the New Freedom. Its chief editors were Herbert Croly, Walter Lippmann and Walter Weyl.

In the intellectual world, in philosophy and in the social sciences, a new, positive, optimistic approach to life developed. In the previous half-century Darwinism, with its theory of evolution as applied to living things, had led to Social Darwinism. Seizing primarily on the idea of "the survival of the fittest," the Social Darwinists used their theories to justify the world as it was. If the fittest survive, then those who have achieved the most power, control the biggest businesses and have the most money must be the fittest. Finally, therefore, they are entitled to what they have grabbed and it is impossible to do anything about this because it involves the workings of "natural law."

Now there appeared men who questioned this deterministic view of organized society, its economy and its political systems. Inspired partly by the basic American optimism that progress was inevitable, and partly by scientific and technological advances which showed that it was possible for man to control a great deal of his natural environment, they asked why man could not control and improve his social environment also.

There were, however, men of the older generation who were influential and who did not share this optimism. Such a man was William Graham Sumner (1840–1910) who, from his Yale professorship, greatly affected the thought of the time about economics, political science and sociology. In *Folkways* (1907) he sought to show that custom was the underlying factor that formed the basis of all institutions. Henry Adams (1838–1918), trained as a historian, was sceptical and pessimistic. He contrasted the order and unity of the Middle

Ages (in *Mont-Saint-Michel and Chartres,* 1904) with the twentieth-century's multiplicity (in *The Education of Henry Adams,* 1907). In one he saw the Virgin Mary as the object of worship, in the other, the dynamo. He wrote in *The Education:*

> The child born in 1900 would, then, be born into a new world which would not be a unity but a multiple. Adams tried to imagine it, and an education that would fit it. He found himself in a land where no one had ever penetrated before; where order was an accidental relation obnoxious to nature; artificial compulsion imposed on motion; against which every free energy of the universe revolted; and which, being merely occasional, resolved itself back into anarchy at last.

Two men of different generations who took a more hopeful attitude toward the modern world, although they differed on many points, were the veteran jurist, Oliver Wendell Holmes (1841–1935), and the young writer on political affairs, Walter Lippmann (1889–). Holmes, already recognized as a distinguished judge and man of intellectual stature, was appointed to the United States Supreme Court by President Roosevelt in 1902 when he was sixty-one years old. Holmes became known as "the great dissenter" because he often disagreed with his more conventional and conservative colleagues. His notable contributions, in these dissents and elsewhere, were his clear and forceful arguments that law was not something imposed by nature which stood the same for all time—something that man neither could nor should tamper with. Holmes's sparse clear prose argued that the law at any given time was what the ruling group in society wanted it to be. It was whatever suited the moral and political theories of the time, and it was even in part nothing more than the prejudices of judges, who reflected the attitudes of their fellow citizens. Holmes's voice was an encouraging one to those who thought man should deal with facts, not theories, and should get on with the business of changing the world. Holmes himself was not at all sure that the world was very easy to reform.

Lippmann was one of the bright young men who were active in public affairs under leaders such as Roosevelt and Wilson. His first book, *A Preface to Politics* appeared when he was only twenty-four. In 1914 in *Drift and Mastery,* Lippmann argued with the energy of youth that man no longer needed to let the political and economic world drift. It was now possible to take steps to master the world, to impose a rational plan on civilization.

There were rebels and innovators in economics, anthropology and history also. Thorstein Veblen (1857–1929) never could fit into the normal pattern of academic life, but he made a greater impact than most of his more conventional colleagues. He delighted in shocking his readers with his unorthodox views, as in *The Theory of the Leisure Class* (1899) where he flayed the crassness of the rich and made popular such phrases as "conspicuous consumption" and "conspicuous waste." In *The Theory of Business Enterprise* (1904) he attacked the businessman who seeks control of industrial enterprises solely to make money, contrasting him with the engineers and managers who are interested in producing goods, and are therefore doing something useful for society.

Franz Boas (1858–1942), German-born scholar who taught at Columbia University for over forty years, was the author of numerous scholarly monographs and his research and fieldwork made anthropology a modern science. His influence on the layman and on the changing temper of the times came more through *The Mind of Primitive Man* (1911) than any other book. Here was the best argument yet against the idea that "race" determines ability and that nothing can be done about it.

There were challenges to the old ways of studying and writing history, especially in the work of James Harvey Robinson (1863–1936) and Charles A. Beard (1874–1948). They collaborated on a textbook in 1907, *The Development of Modern Europe.* In it they stressed their argument that history should justify itself by being made useful for the present. They believed economic matters, such as the Industrial Revolution, should receive far more attention at the expense of the old-fashioned history that emphasized wars and political affairs. In 1912 Robinson published *The New History* to explain and defend his view of how historians should operate. Beard, in 1913, shocked many people with his book, *An Economic Interpretation of the Constitution,* in which he sought to show that the Constitution of the United States reflected the economic interests of the men who wrote it, most of them being well-to-do. In 1917 Beard resigned his Columbia professorship to protest the dismissal of other professors who opposed America's entry into World War I.

America's most important contribution to the intellectual world of the first part of the century was the philosophy of pragmatism. This approach to philosophic reasoning got its start in the last quarter of the nineteenth century, especially in the work of Charles S. Peirce (1839–1914). Its most important advocate in the early twentieth century was William James (1842–1919), brother of the novelist Henry James. Already famous for his brilliant *Principles of Psychology,* James stated in his *Pragmatism* (1907) the central ideas of pragmatism, making them known to a larger circle. It also influenced John Dewey (1859–1952) and, largely through him, pragmatism affected the thinking of scholars in many fields. Its most observable effect was in education.

Pragmatism was a philosophy well-suited to the progressive era. Unlike Darwinism, it said that it was possible for man to exercise some control over events. It was experimental and insisted on investigation rather than reliance on reasoning alone. Basically, its thesis was that the truth and value of ideas should be judged by their outcome—whether they lead to any practical results. The goal was knowledge that contributed to human values. The new mood in political reform, in the writing of history and in other walks of life was receptive to such a practical philosophy.

The man who came to be most closely identified with pragmatism was John Dewey, who was born in Vermont and taught at a number of universities, particularly at Columbia, where he was a familiar figure for many years. He became interested in education above all else, and *The School and Society* (1899) inaugurated his reign over educational theory. He thought education at the time was hopelessly out of touch with reality. He wanted school and real life to relate to each other. From his theories came progressive education, often attacked as "sparing the rod and spoiling the child." It was, though, the only comprehensive attempt to put the school system in touch with the twentieth-century world.

Dewey, along with other scholars and writers of the time, showed that the intellectual world had something to contribute to solving the problems of the new century. Dynamic public figures such as Theodore Roosevelt might attract more attention, but they knew that ideas and action had to go hand in hand.

11 *Art, Music, Drama, Architecture*

THE REFORMING SPIRIT of the progressive movement, the new materials and methods of science and technology, and the general atmosphere of the crowded urban world had their effects on the arts. New movements in art began in France: Fauvism, from about 1905 to 1908, was expressed in vivid colors and strong distortions of form; Cubism, starting in 1909, involved the changing of natural forms into abstract arrangements. About 1904 young artists in France and Germany became aware of primitive art, especially African Negro sculpture. In the United States it was significant that a number of the younger artists began as artist-journalists and newspaper illustrators, dealing with the everyday world as it was.

There was less experimentation in music, but there was a growing interest in it. Playwrights and producers had already begun to throw off the shackles and traditions of the polite theater, and to present plays that criticized the real world. Architecture, most of all, reflected the possibilities of technology and the problems of the urban and industrial world.

Among the older generation of painters with established reputations, most of whom showed at least some hint of newer trends, were Winslow Homer (1836–1910), Thomas Eakins (1844–1916), Mary Cassatt (1845–1926) and Albert Ryder (1847–1917). Homer concentrated more and more on watercolors of sea scenes while Eakins was known for his realistic oil paintings of American life, especially of athletes and athletic events. Miss Cassatt used the impressionistic style for her many pleasing portrayals of her favorite subject, motherhood. Ryder's rather mysterious scenes, in which the moon often played a part, evoked a mood of brooding and mystery.

At this same time a newer generation of artists appeared on the American scene. They were realists, concerned with their contemporary world. One group, known as "The Eight," exemplified them, while their style and subject matter earned them the title of the "Ashcan School." Robert Henri (1865–1929) was the leader around whom they united to form this group, in 1908, in order to put on an exhibit of their work, which more conservative artists and critics deplored. Henri's most important contribution turned out to be his influence as a teacher of others, but he was a fine portrait painter.

Among The Eight were Maurice Prendergast (1859–1924), Ernest Lawson (1873–1939) and William Glackens (1870–1938). These three were impressionistic in style and all specialized in landscapes and contemporary scenes. Arthur B. Davies (1862–1928) painted more romantic pictures of idyllic landscapes. Everett Shinn (1876–1953) was a successful magazine illustrator who also painted street scenes and views of theatrical life. George Luks (1867–1933) and John Sloan (1871–1951) were both newspaper artists as well as painters, and both delighted in showing the world and its people as they were. All of The Eight rebelled against the pretty but insipid pictures of the older, established academic school of painting. To the disappointment of some of the critics, their 1908 exhibit was a popular success. The Eight also made other American artists aware of the life around them. They brought to art a new vitality, and proved that everyday scenes showing ordinary people could be worthy subjects for the painter, even if this meant painting city backyards, crowded business streets, and the loneliness of the city at night.

Among other artists, some of them still younger than The Eight, who became prominent in these years, was Marsden Hartley (1877–1943), known best for his paintings of Maine people and scenery. Arthur Dove (1880–1946) took up an abstract style while Max Weber (1881–1961), born in Russia, was influenced first by Fauvism and then by Cubism. George Bellows (1882–1925) studied under Henri and his early work had much in common with The Eight. His paintings were realistic and show much feeling for the human race. One of the first artists to draw ideas from the shapes and designs of modern industry was Charles Demuth (1883–1935), while Charles Sheeler (1883–1965) translated such forms, and others, into simpler planes.

The foremost American sculptor of the early years of the century was Augustus Saint-Gaudens (1848–1907), who created some of the nation's largest and best-known statues of public figures. Daniel Chester French (1850–1931) also did memorial statues, his best-known work being the giant-size figure of the seated Abraham Lincoln for the Lincoln Memorial in Washington, D. C. George Grey Barnard (1863–1938), besides being a sculptor, was a collector of medieval art and his collection eventually became the Cloisters, in northern Manhattan. A younger sculptor who later became a leading figure in his field was Jo Davidson (1883–1946).

Alfred Stieglitz (1864–1946) deserves as much credit as any one individual for making the new trends in art known to the public. He was also among the first to treat photography as a fine art. In 1905 he established his Gallery 291, so-called because it was located at 291 Fifth Avenue in New York City. Here he introduced to Americans the leading French artists such as Cézanne, Picasso and Brancusi. He also publicized the work of some of the American artists already mentioned, and others such as John Marin (1870–1953) and Georgia O'Keeffe (1887–). Marin specialized in watercolors and he is remembered most for his Maine seascapes. Miss O'Keeffe, whom Stieglitz married, combined strong clear colors with her background of the Southwest where she did much of her work.

The art event of the period that made the greatest impact on the public, and that did the most to destroy the older artistic standards, was the Armory Show, which opened in New York in February, 1913, and got its name by being held in an armory at Lexington Avenue and Twenty-sixth Street. At first the exhibition was planned to give younger modern artists a place to show their work that the conservative art organizations would not exhibit. The Eight rather dominated the early plans. Then it was decided more attention could be secured if works of some contemporary European artists were also included. When the show opened it contained about 1,600 paintings and sculptures, among them work by Manet, Monet, Van Gogh and Seurat.

The show was an immediate sensation, drawing large crowds and also much criticism. Most of the art critics were horrified, using such words as "pathological," "hideous" and "subversive." Much ridicule was heaped on Marcel Duchamp's cubistic painting, "Nude Descending a Staircase," which one commentator called an "explosion in a shingle factory." Ex-President Roosevelt came and wrote a review of the show for *Outlook* magazine. He tried to be sympathetic, for he always liked new things and new ideas, but he qualified his general friendliness with the observation that there was "apt to be a lunatic fringe among the votaries of any forward movement." As the Armory Show became talked about, people came in ever-larger numbers. They also began to buy the paintings, although they spent more on the Europeans' work than on that of the Americans for whom the show had originally been planned. The Armory Show was also seen in Boston and Chicago (where the Law and Order League unsuccessfully demanded that it be closed). In all about half a million people attended the exhibit which introduced large numbers of the American public to twentieth-century art.

There were many musicians in the United States, some professionals and some amateurs, some teachers and some students, but America looked to Europe for musical leadership. It seemed as though one had to be born on the Continent to achieve the top rungs of the musical ladder in this country. There were only nine symphony orchestras in the whole nation in 1900, and only five of these were professional. Americans in a few large cities could, however, hear the best the world had to offer. Late in 1903 the Italian tenor, Enrico Caruso (1873–1921), made his American debut at the Metropolitan Opera House in New York in *Rigoletto,* and before the end of the year the Met staged Wagner's *Parsifal,* the first scenic performance of it outside Bayreuth. When the Met presented Strauss's *Salome* in 1907 it found itself the center of such a storm of protest that it withdrew the production. The famous dance in the opera was considered scandalous by those who ruled New York's morals at the time, while one critic said the music was excellent but was used to "sicken the mind and wreck the nerves." That same year Feodor Chaliapin, the Russian basso, and Mary Garden, Scottish-born soprano, made their American debuts.

The Irish tenor John McCormack (1884–1945) first sang in America in 1909 and remained extremely popular for many years. Leopold Stokowski (1882–   ), born in London, became director of the Philadelphia Orchestra in 1912 and held the post for a quarter of a century. The following year Italian-born Arturo Toscanini (1867–1957) made his American bow as a symphony conductor, although he had begun conducting operatic performances at the Metropolitan Opera in 1908. Here he led the American premiere of Puccini's *Girl of the Golden West.* About a quarter of a century later Toscanini moved permanently to the United States. Jean Sibelius, the Finnish composer, came to America in 1914 to conduct the world premiere of one of his compositions, while Jascha Heifetz, the violinist, first appeared here in 1917. The Russian-born musician, who later became an American citizen, was only sixteen years old at the time. Walter Damrosch (1862–1950) was born in Germany but spent almost all his life here, conducting and composing for many years. He led the Metropolitan Opera orchestra, as had his father before him, and his own opera, *Cyrano,* was performed there in 1913. Damrosch later was one of the first musicians to see the educational possibilities of radio.

There were few American composers of serious music, at least of music that was accepted and performed. Charles Ives (1874–1954) was composing at this time in an advanced style, but his works were not published or played. In 1939 when his piano sonata, "Concord," was performed, he finally received recognition. "Concord" was composed between 1909 and 1915. Much more successful were Ethelbert Nevin (1862–1901) and Charles Wakefield Cadman (1881–1946). Nevin's two most popular pieces were composed before the turn of the century, but were among the favorite numbers of amateur singers and pianists for many years after. One of these was "The Rosary," which sold 6,000,000 copies in its first 30 years; the other, the favorite of would-be piano virtuosos, was "Narcissus." Cadman's popular works were equally romantic and sentimental: "At Dawning," written in 1906, and "From the Land of the Sky Blue Water" (1909). Cadman made considerable use of American Indian themes.

In the field of the dance, the most successful male performer of the period was a Russian, while America contributed a unique dancer of great talent. The man, who has been called the greatest dancer of all time, was Vaslav Nijinsky of the Ballet Russe who first appeared in the United States in 1916. The American was Isadora Duncan (1878–1927) who had little success at first in her homeland. Beginning in 1903 she had many triumphs in Europe and, in 1908, America accepted her with enthusiasm. She pioneered in expressionism and had permanent influence on the dance of the twentieth century. She performed barefoot, wearing a tunic adapted from the Greek style, and scarves.

The theater was busy and prosperous in the prewar years. There was no competition from radio or television, but the movies were a growing competitor for the entertainment seeker's dollar. Many clever drawing-room comedies and run-of-the-mill dramas were staged, but new forces were invading the world of the playwright and the actor. Naturalism and symbolism were the coming styles in the theater; plays were concerned with serious personal and social problems; and, as in music and art, Europe was showing the way to the more innocent and provincial Americans. Most of the plays of Henrik Ibsen, the Norwegian playwright, were written before 1900 but they exerted great influence on the twentieth-century stage. *A Doll's House* shocked New York audiences when it was presented in 1907. In the 1905–06 season, six of George Bernard Shaw's plays were produced on Broadway and the irreverent Irish playwright also shocked people with his witty views on morals and politics. *Mrs. Warren's Profession* was closed by the police as immoral. At the same time people were flocking to applaud Maude Adams in the fantasy, *Peter Pan.* One New York seamstress reportedly saw it forty-seven times to escape from her own dull life. Miss Adams (1872–1953) was one of the most popular actresses of the day, starring in *Quality Street* in 1901 and in *What Every Woman Knows* in 1908.

John Drew (1853–1927), a handsome, romantic type who was especially good in comedy, was one of the very popular actors of the time. So also was Otis Skinner (1858–1942), who in 1911 won lasting fame playing the leading role in *Kismet,* an Oriental fantasy. Mrs. Minnie Maddern Fiske (1865–1932) showed unusual talent in a number of Ibsen plays, but was best liked in lighter productions, such as *Salvation Nell* in 1908. David Warfield (1866–1951) first demonstrated his talent in *The Auctioneer* (1901). He is remembered most of all, though, for his sympathetic portrayal of a self-sacrificing man in *The Music Master,* which opened in 1904 and ran for three years in New York and on tour. The Barrymore family became the first family of the American theater. Lionel (1878–1954) was an excellent character actor, both on the stage and in the movies. His sister, Ethel (1879–1959), was an immediate success in 1901 when she appeared in *Captain Jinks of the Horse Marines.* Their younger brother, John (1882–1942), more than handsome enough to become a matinee idol, was gushed over by millions of girls and women. Most of his work after 1912 was in the movies.

The most successful and most prolific playwright of the time was Clyde Fitch (1865–1909) who wrote thirty-six plays in his forty-four years (including *Captain Jinks*). His best works, such as *The Truth* (1907) and *The City* (1909), reflected American life of his day. Edward Sheldon (1886–1946) had his first success when he was only twenty-two, with *Salvation Nell.* His most popular play, though, was *Romance* in 1913. William Vaughan Moody wrote serious social drama, such as *The Great Divide,* a success in 1906, and *The Faith Heale*r (1909). Israel Zangwill (1864–1926), Jewish novelist and playwright, brought to the stage a subject that was of concern in other fields when he wrote *The Melting Pot,* a study of Jewish immigrant life in the United States which was produced in 1908.

Theater groups were active. The Irish Players from the Abbey Theater, Dublin, first visited the United States in 1911 and offered plays such as J. M. Synge's controversial *The Playboy of the Western World.* In 1915 the Washington Square Players, a group that later became the Theater Guild, gave its first season of one-act plays. The following year the Provincetown Players organized and staged plays both at Provincetown on Cape Cod and in New York. They introduced to the world the work of Eugene O'Neill (1888–1953), America's most talented playwright, beginning with his one-act piece, *Bound East for Cardiff,* in 1916.

In no area of fine or applied arts was there a closer relationship among the spirit of the twentieth century, the accelerating urbanization, and the latest technology, than in architecture. The skyscraper towering over the city became a symbol of the new century and the new America. Its roots, however, were firmly in the late nineteenth century, when electric lighting was developed so that window areas became less important, when the electric elevator was invented, and, most of all, when the steel skeleton, capable of sustaining both floors and walls, was perfected. Chicago was the birthplace of the modern steel skyscraper, although it was in New York that the tallest ones were constructed.

America also had some architects who held to older styles and who built some of the nation's most impressive structures. Charles F. McKim (1847–1909), of the leading firm of McKim, Mead and White, held to classic and renaissance styles. Some of the largest railroad stations were being built and the classic style was an ideal one when the problem was to cover a large area with a relatively low building designed in an ornate manner. McKim's firm designed Pennsylvania Station in New York, which was erected between 1906 and 1910, at the same time that tunnels were dug under the Hudson River to bring trains directly into Manhattan from the west. The president of the Pennsylvania Railroad who conceived the whole project was Alexander Cassatt, brother of the painter Mary Cassatt. The great hall of the station copied the imperial Roman bath of the Emperor Caracalla. McKim was also responsible for the equally impressive and classical Grand Central Terminal in New York, the construction of which ran from 1903 to 1913. In 1902, at the request of President and Mrs. Roosevelt, McKim managed a project to restore the White House to its proper glory and he also designed one of New York's landmarks, the Morgan Library on East Thirty-sixth Street.

Stanford White (1853–1906), the third name in McKim's firm, specialized in the decorative elements of architecture. He designed some elegant and luxurious city and country houses in such places as New York and Newport, and those that still stand are a delight to the eye, both inside and out. He also designed such handsome structures as the Century Club in New York. Ralph Adams Cram (1863–1942) represented the architects who favored the Gothic style. He designed a number of college buildings and churches in this manner, the one most favored for such structures, and he converted the unfinished Cathedral of St. John the Divine in New York from the Romanesque to the Gothic.

Although he belonged to the same generation as men such as McKim, Louis Henry Sullivan (1856–1924) took an entirely different path. He wanted to leave the older styles behind and to develop an American style. He believed that the form of a building should express its function, not try to hide it. A bank should not look like a Greek temple, he felt, but like one of the small banks he designed, such as the National Farmers' Bank (1908) in Owatonna, Minnesota. While Sullivan did not invent the steel skeleton skyscraper, he did more before 1900 than anyone else to make it practical and accepted.

Another pioneer in modern business building design was Daniel E. Burnham (1846–1912). Besides structures in Chicago, he designed one of New York's landmarks, the Flatiron Building, 22 stories and 180 feet high, constructed between 1902 and 1904 on a triangular plot where Broadway and Fifth Avenue cross. In 1901 Burnham became chairman of a commission to plan an ordered development of Washington, D. C. Out of this grew the civic-planning movement and Burnham became a leader in the field. He did city planning for other cities, including Chicago. As part of his work in Washington he designed the handsome Union Station (1904) in classic style to match the Capitol and other government buildings.

The Flatiron Building held its title as the tallest skyscraper for only a few years. In 1908 the Singer Building in lower Manhattan reached a new high of 612 feet. Designed by Ernest Flagg, it was topped by an ornamented dome that had dormer windows and a copper turret. Tourists paid fifty cents to go up to the fortieth floor observation area. The Singer Building's triumph was short-lived; before the year was out the Metropolitan Life Tower, on Madison Square, went up to 700 feet. It was designed by Napoleon LeBrun who started the tower upward as a strikingly modern plain shaft, but when he got to the top he ended it with several layers of Grecian architectural elements. Cass Gilbert (1859–1934), one of the most versatile and successful architects of his time, designed the building that held the title of tallest skyscraper until 1930. This was the Woolworth Building, in lower Manhattan, a distinguished Gothic-ornamented tower that remains the proudest symbol of the age of the early skyscrapers. It was completed in 1913, rising to a height of 55 stories and 760½ feet.

The most talented and influential architect of the period—and for many years afterward—was Frank Lloyd Wright (1869–1959), who was a student of Sullivan. He designed houses that were low, with horizontal lines that, he said, matched the prairie. They had more open space inside than the traditional houses of the time. One of his early works was the Willitts House at Highland Park, Illinois, in 1902. In the Unity Church in Oak Park, Illinois, in 1903, he showed that concrete could be used successfully in well-designed buildings, and so made the material generally acceptable. He also pioneered in modern office structures such as the Larkin Building in Buffalo in 1904.

Wright was an innovator in his field in tune with the forward thrust of the times, as were Theodore Dreiser, Robert Henri, Charles Ives and Eugene O'Neill in theirs. None succeeded in achieving perfection, anymore than Theodore Roosevelt or Woodrow Wilson did in government, but all were united in seeking something other than what had gone before, in trying to change and improve some aspect of the world they inherited.

12 *Fun and Games*

AMERICANS WERE in the process of throwing off some of the old restraints on entertainment and recreation as the twentieth century began. It was a gradual process, now accelerated considerably by the continental European immigrants whose attitudes were less austere than the Puritan New England heritage that had hitherto dominated America.

On farms and in small towns there was not much organized or professional entertainment. Hunting and fishing were easily available for boys and men, although many complained that fish and game were not as plentiful as they once were. There were church socials, and Fourth of July parades, with picnics and speeches. In these events, as in many a winter evening gathering, people entertained themselves with games and singing. In the cities, more professional entertainment was available for those who had the money. Baseball and boxing were the main professional sports. There was also a great deal of popular theatrical activity—plays and vaudeville.

The rich went to Europe, or to the mountains or the seashore for the summer, but most people could not get away, and if they had any time off they could not afford to travel very far. At the same time, public recreational facilities such as parks, tennis courts and golf links were almost unknown. Ocean or lake beaches were popular with the common people of cities fortunate enough to have such things. One popular spectacle of the time was the balloon race which, as part of a county fair or other gathering, attracted large crowds. The exposition which opened in St. Louis, Missouri, in 1904 in celebration of the hundredth anniversary of the Louisiana Purchase was the kind of event that drew visitors from all over the country. This one also gave the nation an enduring song, "Meet Me in St. Louis, Louis."

As the century grew slightly older, technology, for the first time in history, began to play an important part in the world of entertainment. It started to separate the performer from the viewer or listener, to turn former participants into passive spectators. The two products of technology which began this trend were the phonograph and the movies.

Americans have always liked humor, even though it has seemed to some observers that humor of a rather low and loud type is preferred. The favorite humorist of the early 1900's was Finley Peter Dunne (1867–1936) whose dialogues, in Irish-American dialect, featured "Mr. Dooley," the saloon-keeper. On the matter of dealing with the insurrectionists in the Philippines after the Spanish-American War, "Mr. Dooley" observed:

> Whin we plant what Hogan calls th' starry banner iv Freedom in th' Ph'lippeens, an' give th' sacred blessin' iv liberty to the poor, downtrodden people iv thim unfortunate isles,—dam thim!—we'll larn thim a lesson. . . . So I suppose, Hinnissy, we'll have to stay an' do th' best we can. . . . They'se wan consolation; an' that is, if th' American people can govern thimsilves, they can govern anything that walks.

One new form of humor—one is tempted to say a new art form —devised by Americans about this time was the comic strip. It began with "The Yellow Kid" in the 1890's. Soon, instead of single cartoons, there were strips showing and telling a story, and more of them were printed in color. The "funnies" became one of the most popular features of the Sunday newspaper. There was "Happy Hooligan,"

"The Katzenjammer Kids" (which contributed the word "nix" to the language), "Buster Brown" with his dog, and "Little Nemo," created by Winsor McCay in a fanciful Art Nouveau style that, when looked at today, seems an obvious source of inspiration for the Beatles' "Yellow Submarine." The original daily comic strip, "Mutt and Jeff," began in 1907; "Bringing Up Father" arrived in 1913 to tell the first husband and wife cartoon story. "Krazy Kat," drawn by George Herriman, was in some not quite definable way unique both in style and in characters, such as Ignatz the mouse and Offisa Bull Pupp the dog.

Baseball was truly the national sport. It attracted more spectators and more enthusiasm than any other pastime, and it was also the most common sport of boys on vacant lots in small towns and large cities alike. One league of professional teams, the National League, had been in existence for a quarter of a century. In 1900 eager promoters turned the Western League into the American League and by 1903 its older brother recognized it as an equal and the first World Series between the two league champions was played. Boston of the American League defeated Pittsburgh of the National League.

The glamorous names of baseball began to appear. Connie Mack, who lasted until after World War II, became the manager of the Philadelphia Athletics in 1901, while in the following year John J. McGraw, known as the "Little Napoleon," was hired as manager of the New York Giants, a post he held for thirty years. Two years later his team haughtily refused to play Boston in the World Series, not being willing to concede that the American League was the equal of the National. The Giants' greatest pitcher was Christy Mathewson, who in the 1905 World Series pitched three shutouts, a feat still unequalled. The best all-around player of the period was Ty Cobb of Detroit who won the American League batting championship every year between 1910 and 1919, except for 1916 when an almost equally fine player, Tris Speaker, came out ahead. The sport's greatest hero,

Babe Ruth, entered the major leagues in 1914 when he joined the Boston Red Sox. He first won fame as a pitcher before becoming the leading home-run hitter of the game's entire history. Boys and men eagerly collected pictures of their favorite players which were to be found in cigarette packages.

Boxing was much less respectable than baseball, and was illegal in many areas. It had its avid followers, however, and some of its most popular champions in this period. There also arose for the first time in sports the element of black versus white. James J. Jeffries won the heavyweight boxing title in 1899 and he retained it until 1905 when he retired undefeated. Late in 1908, in far-off Sydney, Australia, an American Negro, Jack Johnson, defeated Tommy Burns, a Canadian, and claimed the title. Two years later Jeffries came out of retirement, fought Johnson and lost to make Johnson the first Negro champion. The fight caused some controversy beforehand when the Governor of California forced it out of the state. It was held in Reno, Nevada. There was some scarcely subdued race feeling afterwards. Five years later a "white hope," young Jess Willard, knocked out Johnson to win the title. This fight had to be held in Havana, Cuba, to escape anti-boxing laws.

There was no professional football but the game was played in colleges from coast to coast. However, to read the newspapers and to look at the all-American teams, one would think that the game was played only in the East, and played well only at the Ivy League colleges. Yale was conceded to be the best team in the nation in 1900 because it had beaten Harvard and Princeton, while every member of that year's all-American eleven was from the East and all but two were from the Ivy League. Here the games were just as important as social affairs as they were as sport. Papers ran separate articles on the society figures who attended and in 1905 it took fifty special parlor cars to transport society's contingent to New Haven for the Yale game with Princeton. Football then was a rough game of flying wedges and sweaty pile-ups. No forward passing was allowed. That energetic sportsman President Roosevelt intervened in 1905 to have the rules changed because injuries were becoming too numerous.

Golf and tennis were played almost entirely by ladies and gentlemen of some means and considerable leisure. Both games were considered somewhat sissified. The major tennis tournament was played as a matter of course at the fashionable summer resort of Newport. It was quite a triumph for the United States when the American May Sutton won the English women's lawn tennis championship in 1907. Most of the golf professionals then making a living from the game were Scotch, but in 1913 a former caddy, Francis Ouimet, won the open championship, defeating the pros and the gentlemanly amateurs. The greatest all-around American athlete of the time, and perhaps of all time, was Jim Thorpe. Part Indian, he played football for the Carlisle Indian School when it shocked the sporting world by defeating mighty Harvard. In the 1912 Olympic Games Thorpe won both the pentathlon and the decathlon and received worldwide acclaim. A few months later he was required to return his medals when it was discovered that he had previously violated his amateur standing by briefly playing semi-professional baseball.

With no radio or television to keep people at home, light theatrical entertainment, the musical comedy and vaudeville all enjoyed prosperity. The century opened with one of its most successful musical comedies, *Floradora,* featuring the six "Floradora girls," whose charms enchanted all New York. According to tradition, every one of them married a millionaire. The year 1903 was marked by George M. Cohan's appearance in a musical comedy of his own, and by the success of Victor Herbert's first operetta, *Babes in Toyland.* A fabulous theater that all visitors to New York felt they had to see opened in 1905. It was the Hippodrome, which featured extravagant spectacles of players and costumes, particularly the dancing girls who seemed to disappear into an enormous tank of water. The next year Cohan produced one of his most popular shows, *Forty-Five Minutes from Broadway* with co-star Fay Templeton. At another theater Anna Held and her songs were the toast of Broadway. The first of a long series of *Ziegfeld Follies,* staged by Florenz Ziegfeld and always featuring "the most beautiful girls in the world," was successful in 1907, and at a cost of only $13,000.

Oscar Straus's *The Chocolate Soldier* was one of the hits of 1909; the next year there was Victor Herbert's *Naughty Marietta,* which introduced "Ah, Sweet Mystery of Life." That same year Fanny Brice made her debut on Broadway in the new edition of the *Ziegfeld Follies.* The Follies led the way again in 1917 when it included in its cast two up-and-coming comedians, Will Rogers and Eddie Cantor, along with such beautiful girls as Billie Dove, Mae Murray and Marion Davies. It was now the year America entered World War I and so one of the female singers brought down the final curtain by appearing as Columbia, wrapped in an American flag.

Vaudeville at this time was entertaining thousands of Americans because it could be seen all over the country in theaters in medium-sized cities. Also, it had grown respectable and attractive. For twenty-five cents at the most a patron could enjoy a wide variety of acts: comedians, singers, dancers, magicians, trained animals and performers of all kinds from New York and Europe. Eva Tanguay, Nora Bayes, Sophie Tucker and the Dolly Sisters were popular, along with Annette Kellerman, of the "perfect" figure, who achieved fame by appearing in a one-piece bathing suit. Harry Houdini became the greatest magician of all. Comedians who had audiences slapping their knees were Ed Wynn and Leon Erroll, who appeared on the first bill to play the Palace Theater when it opened on Broadway in 1913. For two decades every vaudevillian's highest ambition was to play the Palace. A much-imitated comedy team was Moran and Mack (the Two Black Crows). From Scotland came a star of the English music-halls, Harry Lauder, singing such songs as "Roamin' in the Gloamin'."

Many of the popular songs written during the period are still sung and played today. In the titles of these songs can be found clues to the events and interests of Americans in the progressive era. New inventions, for example, inspired a number of songs, such as: "Hello, Central, Give Me Heaven, for My Mamma's There," "Come, Josephine, in My Flying Machine," "In My Merry Oldsmobile," and "He'd Have to Get Under" (subtitled "Get out and Get Under to Fix up His Automobile"). Songs with an Indian theme, such as "Hiawatha," were well thought of. The change in the status and condition of the Negro was reflected in popular music. He was no longer associated with the southern plantation type of song, such as "Old Black Joe," but with a more independent, citified atmosphere. Nevertheless, songs about Negroes pictured them as living in a different, inferior world and as objects of fun, like children, innocent but ignorant. From this approach came such songs as "Bill Bailey, Won't You Please Come Home," "What You Goin' to Do When the Rent Comes 'Round," and "The Darktown Strutters Ball."

Two of the most successful song writers of the time were Harry Von Tilzer and Paul Dresser. The former wrote more than 3,000 songs in all. Most of them have long since been forgotten, but some are still remembered: "A Bird in a Gilded Cage," "Wait Till the Sun Shines Nelly," "Under the Yum Yum Tree," "On a Sunday Afternoon," "The Beautiful Sea," "In the Evening by the Moonlight," and "I Want a Girl Just Like the Girl That Married Dear Old Dad." Paul Dresser was the brother of novelist Theodore Dreiser, having changed the spelling of his name. He was one of the best known and liveliest members of the Broadway night-life crowd. Today he is best recalled by "My Gal Sal."

There were so many hit songs of the era that it would take pages to name them all. Many had a nostalgic air, a yearning for childhood and the country: "In the Good Old Summer Time," "In the Shade of the Old Apple Tree," "Sweet Adeline," "Little Grey Home in the West," "School Days," "Down by the Old Mill Stream," "Let Me Call You Sweetheart," "Shine on, Harvest Moon," "Good-Bye, Dolly Gray," "Put on Your Old Grey Bonnet," and "Take Me Out to the Ball Game." The most successful writer of the really sentimental song was Carrie Jacobs Bond with "Just a-Wearyin' for You," "I Love You Truly," and "A Perfect Day."

There were also songs that were soon forgotten, such as: "The Bird on Nellie's Hat," "Don't Put Me Off at Buffalo Any More," "A Lemon in the Garden of Love," "When You Know You're Not Forgotten by the Girl You Can't Forget," "She's the Fairest Little Flower Dear Old Dixie Ever Grew," and "Fido Is a Hot Dog Now."

Toward the end of the period songs appeared that heralded events to come. "There's a Long Long Trail" (1913) and "Keep the Home Fires Burning" (1915) were soon to be forever associated with war. On the other hand, W. C. Handy's "St. Louis Blues" in 1914 and the Original Dixieland Jazz Band's "Tiger Rag" in 1917 helped usher in new styles in popular music—blues and jazz. Before that, however, there was ragtime, a forerunner of jazz, that was best exhibited by a syncopated piano style. "Alexander's Ragtime Band," written in 1911 by a promising twenty-three-year-old songwriter named Irving Berlin, was the most popular and the most typical of the ragtime numbers. Another long-lasting piece was "Maple Leaf Rag." At this same time a precocious teenager, Duke Ellington, was making his musical start as a ragtime pianist in Washington.

The rhythm of ragtime helped bring about a revolution in dancing also. Faster and less inhibited dancing was required of the couples who did the bunny hug and the turkey trot. The tango was another new favorite. The height of the dance craze came in the years after 1913 and received its greatest impetus from the attractive young dance team of Vernon and Irene Castle. They made their debut as a team in a musical comedy in 1913, in which they did the turkey trot and the tango. The waltz at once dropped in popularity, although the Castles liked to perform the "hesitation waltz." They later introduced the fox trot, which had more lasting popularity than some other dances of the time, such as the Castle Walk and the maxixe for which they were briefly famous. The Castles' popularity was as much the result of their youthful charm as it was of their dancing ability. Vernon was handsome and made all young men want to be as slim and graceful as he was. Irene was slim, too, and she is credited with having ended the reign of the curvier silhouette made famous by such belles as Lillian Russell. Irene also had something to do with raising skirts a little off the floor, but her influence over America's women was shown most clearly when she bobbed her hair. Thousands of other girls at once adopted this daring style, including the black velvet headband, known to those who didn't like it as a "headache band." Vernon, an Englishman, died in a plane crash in Texas in 1918 while teaching American army pilots how to fly. Irene lived until 1969 but her dancing days were over.

Whether for singing or dancing, those who wanted popular music had to create it themselves for the most part, or go to a theater or place of entertainment where a live orchestra performed. The piano and sheet music, present in nearly every home, were the basis of private musical fun. There was also the player piano, while the phonograph, invented a quarter century back, was just beginning to become practical. In 1903 an American company began to issue recordings of opera stars, who sang with only a piano accompaniment. Orchestral recordings were not attempted until about 1913. A machine which was to give its name to phonographs in general, the hand-wound Victrola, was first offered for sale in 1915.

The invention that brought a whole new era of public entertainment was in its infancy in 1900. This was the motion picture. Before

1900 moving pictures had been seen mostly in slot machines in penny arcades. The first attempts had been made to project the pictures onto a screen and such movies were seen as part of vaudeville shows or in amusement arcades. Then in 1902 in Los Angeles a place was opened for the showing of movies only. This first movie theater was in a store, as were all of them until 1905 when a man in Pittsburgh, Pennsylvania, built the first movie theater. Since the usual price of admission in those days was a nickel, the movies were known as nickelodeons. By 1908 there were 8,000 to 10,000 nickelodeons in the nation with 200,000 persons a day attending them in 550 New York City showplaces alone. Techniques and equipment were both new and unperfected. The pictures were jumpy, scenes could be photographed only in bright daylight, and, of course, the movies were silent. Printed titles and appropriate music played on a piano substituted. Many piano teachers and church organists found work in movie houses.

The first movie that told a story was produced in 1903—*The Great Train Robbery*. There were no stars then, but when Mary Pickford, beginning in 1909, received special attention she became "America's Sweetheart" and the star system was soon the normal way of catching the public's fancy. The movies also moved west and after 1913 Hollywood was the motion picture capital. Serials, which were seen once a week, usually at a Saturday matinee for the children, were popular. Ruth Roland and Pearl White starred in such serials as *The Perils of Pauline,* each installment of which ended with the hero or heroine in a seemingly hopeless situation. Westerns and comedies began to provide standard fare for the moviemakers and the moviegoers. Tom Mix was the ideal hero of the tales of the West. John Bunny and Fatty Arbuckle were early comedians with large followings, while Mack Sennett's Keystone Cops provided the ideal popular combination of comedy and chase. Charlie Chaplin made his first movie in 1914 and was on the way to enormous success. Three years later an almost equally favorite comedian, Harold Lloyd, made his screen debut.

At the same time movies were getting longer, and more attention was paid to story and setting. Camera and other techniques, such as lighting, were improving, and a new profession calling for special talent, that of movie director, developed. Stories such as *The Prisoner of Zenda* and *The Count of Monte Cristo,* were made into movies. Handsome leading men, such as Douglas Fairbanks and Francis X. Bushman, were worshiped from afar by thousands of women. Stars who achieved fame as the motion picture became universal entertainment were Wallace Beery, Gloria Swanson, Wallace Reid, Lillian Gish, Theda Bara, and many others. Among the directors, Cecil B. DeMille and D. W. Griffith became household names. It was DeMille who, with Samuel Goldwyn, produced the first Hollywood feature-length film. This was *The Squaw Man* in 1913. DeMille was among the first to try to use artificial lighting, and he introduced the symbol of the well-equipped movie director—the megaphone. Griffith, who devised the close-up and the flashback among other innovations, made cinema history in 1915 with *The Birth of a Nation.* Based on Thomas Dixon's best-selling novel of ten years before, *The Clansman,* it not only advanced the technique of moviemaking, but also created a film that commented on a controversial subject—the Reconstruction era and the activities of the Ku Klux Klan. It is a landmark of moviemaking, both as to technique and its emotional impact on all who saw it.

In the entertainment world, then, the progressive era offered some of the best of the old and the new. Vaudeville and the theater were soon to start declining. Sports were to take a greater part of the people's time, both as spectators and as participants. Machinery was to play a larger role and to separate the viewer or listener from the performer. At the same time, though, this was to mean that more people could enjoy the fun and the games.

13 *Deeds and Disasters*

THE YEARS BETWEEN 1900 AND 1917 had their share of heroes and villains, of goals successfully reached, of well-meaning efforts that failed, and of disasters beyond the control of man.

The most spectacular triumph of men over nature was also an impressive sign of the new position of the United States as a world power and as a leader in applying the tools and techniques of the machine age. This event was the building of the Panama Canal across Central America to link the Atlantic and Pacific oceans. A French company, headed by the builder of the Suez Canal, Ferdinand de Lesseps, started work on a canal across the Isthmus of Panama in 1881, but gave up in utter defeat in 1889. In the United States there had long been agitation for a canal, either across Panama or across Nicaragua. After the French company reduced its original exorbitant demand for its concession to the still high figure of $40,000,000, Panama became the favored route. However, a half-century-old treaty with Great Britain stood in the way because it provided that neither country could build and control such a canal without the other. In 1901 negotiations resulted in the Hay-Pauncefote Treaty which gave the United States the right to go ahead on its own.

Arrangements also had to be made with Colombia, the nation whose territory included what became the Republic of Panama. A treaty was prepared which would give Colombia $10,000,000 and an annual payment of $250,000 to allow the canal to be built. To America's surprise, Colombia turned down the treaty in 1903. This angered officials in Washington, especially Roosevelt, and it panicked those who stood to gain from the sale of the French company's concession. After some behind-the-scenes intrigue, a revolution took place in Panama. It was quite bloodless and was quietly aided by American warships on hand to see that soldiers of the Colombian government did not land and suppress the revolt. Within a few days, the United States recognized the new nation, and in less than two weeks concluded the Hay-Bunau-Varilla Treaty, with the same terms as those rejected by Colombia.

The methods and actions of the United States in its support of the revolution, and its quick recognition of the new nation, have been criticized ever since. Its dealings with the grasping representatives of the French canal company have also been attacked. In a speech in 1911 Roosevelt used the phrase, "I took the canal." His contention was that if he had not ordered the steps he did, Congress, Colombia and everyone else involved would have debated the issue for months or years, and he believed the construction of the canal at the earliest possible moment was vital for the country. Ten years later the United States paid Colombia $25,000,000 to quiet her claims.

In any event, the United States could start digging the canal. The work was begun by a commission which made some progress but the results did not satisfy impatient President Roosevelt. In 1907 he turned over the job to the Army Corps of Engineers and put George Washington Goethals (1858–1928) in charge. Under Goethals the gigantic project was carried on efficiently. The other man whose name is most associated with the completion of the unprecedented task is William Crawford Gorgas (1854–1920), who had helped conquer yellow fever. He set about successfully ridding the canal area of that disease and protecting the workmen against other tropical diseases and creatures.

The actual digging of the canal, the largest construction project men had ever attempted, centered around three tasks. One was the building of Gatun Dam to harness the Chagres River. The dam was a mile and a half long, 105 feet high and 2,200 feet thick at its base. When finished, it created Gatun Lake with an area of 163 square miles. The most impressive feat was digging through the Continental Divide. In five years men moved a mountain out of the way and the result was the Gaillard Cut. It was named for the Army engineer in charge of the job, David DuBose Gaillard (1859–1913), who ruined his health in the process and died the year the cut was finished. As many as fifty large steam shovels were at work at a time and as much as 1,500,000 cubic yards of earth were removed in a month. By the time the cut was finished, about 80,000,000 cubic yards of earth had been taken out to make a cut 8 miles long, 300 feet wide and 45 feet deep. The third major task in completing the Panama Canal was the construction of locks necessary to raise and lower ships. Six sets of double locks, three at each end, were required. Each was made 1,000 feet long, 110 feet wide and at least 40 feet deep, and in all 4,500,000 cubic yards of concrete were required.

The first ship passed through the Panama Canal in January, 1914, but it was August 15, 1914, before the formal opening took place. By then about 140,000,000 cubic yards of earth in all had been removed and $366,650,000 spent. The canal immediately proved to be a boon to the commerce of all nations, and an important addition to the defense of the United States. The construction of the canal was a triumph of machinery and organization.

In the same period small groups of men were pitting themselves against nature's most extreme cold. During all the centuries, no man had ever set foot at either the North Pole or the South Pole. Now dedicated men were determined to do so. Among these was an American, Robert E. Peary (1856–1920), who had made several attempts to reach the North Pole and on an expedition in 1905–06 had come within about 174 miles of it. He set out on another expedition in 1908. After fighting the elements for many months, Peary, accompanied by four Eskimos and his Negro servant, Matthew Henson, reached the North Pole on April 6, 1909. The trip back was a long one, too, and it was September 6 before he was able to send word by wireless from Labrador that he had achieved his goal. His triumph, though, turned out to have its complications. Peary learned that another American, Frederick A. Cook (1865–1940), claimed he had reached the North Pole a full year before Peary had. For a while Cook had his supporters, but in the end it was generally concluded that his claim was fraudulent. Congress officially recognized Peary as the first man to the pole, and for his achievement made him a rear admiral.

The honor of being the first man at the South Pole went to a Norwegian, Roald Amundsen (1872–1928). He and his fellow explorers, using skis and dog teams, made it to the pole on December 14, 1911, and stayed there for four days. About a month behind Amundsen was the ill-fated Scott expedition, led by the Englishman, Robert F. Scott (1868–1912). He and four companions made their final dash with sledges pulled by hand. They reached the pole on January 18, 1912, only thirty-five days after Amundsen. This disappointment was followed by disaster when all five of the party succumbed to illness, lack of food and the cold on the way back to civilization.

Less spectacular but more important for the world was the work carried on by many different foundations, organizations and movements that began or flourished in this era. Some of the men who had amassed huge fortunes almost by accident as America became industrialized, now began to give away their money in almost equally huge sums. Andrew Carnegie established the Carnegie Corporation in 1911, with an initial $125,000,000 to which he added more later. Carnegie liked especially to donate money for libraries and church organs, but after his death the foundation turned its attention to more general problems of education and aid for underprivileged groups. John D. Rockefeller, Sr., set up a foundation bearing his name in 1913 and gave it $183,000,000 in the first fourteen years. Medical research, education and public health were the fields of most interest. Earlier, the widow of a lesser-known tycoon, Russell Sage, established a foundation in his memory in 1907. Sage had been a banker and as a stock speculator in association with Jay Gould had interests in railroads and in the New York City elevated railway system. Mrs. Stephen V. Harkness, whose husband had been a Rockefeller partner, founded the Commonwealth Fund in 1918. This fund was interested in child-guidance clinics and in rural hospitals.

Social welfare work at this time was performed largely by private organizations, since the Federal government did not enter into this area at all, and state and local governments were not greatly involved. Social work itself was just becoming a profession. Settlement houses, such as Jane Addams's Hull House in Chicago, and the Henry Street Settlement in New York, were already in existence and through funds from private sources offered education and recreation in slum areas. Social surveys were taken to show the extent of such problems as poverty, chronic illness and juvenile delinquency. A movement for parks and playgrounds was beginning to make progress in 1900. By 1915 more than 400 cities had opened such facilities. It was at this time that some concerned citizens began to campaign for more governmental activity and spending for social welfare purposes. They argued that such problems as poverty and juvenile delinquency were the responsibility of the whole community and should not be left to voluntary philanthropy. However, others, including some progressives, still felt that welfare problems should be left to private charity, but the trend of the times was against them.

One of the noisiest, as well as one of the most controversial, movements of the day was the campaign for woman suffrage. There had been agitation about it even before the Civil War and the movement grew stronger after the war. But success was slow in coming. Wyoming in 1869, when it was still a territory, had granted women the right to vote, and most gains had been in the West as part of the Populist reform movement of the late nineteenth century. As time went on, the women became better organized and more vociferous in their agitation. Parades were one of the most popular means of publicizing the campaign. They drew crowds, a large part of which came to make fun of what they considered to be unladylike females. Some men espoused the cause, but the kidding they had to take was discouraging. In New York a parade in 1911 was somewhat of a fiasco —it started late and, of course, everyone said that was just like a bunch of women, even though it wasn't their fault. Another parade on Fifth Avenue the next year was more successful (it started on time) and more impressive. In fact it seemed too successful to the *New York Times* which stuffily editorialized:

> The situation is dangerous. We often hear the remark nowadays that women will get the vote if they try hard enough and persistently; and it is true that they will get it, and play havoc with it for themselves and society, if the men are not firm and wise enough and—it may as well be said—masculine enough to prevent them.

Nevertheless by 1913 about a dozen states had given women the right to vote, and while it was 1920 before this right was recognized in the Federal constitution, women had already come a long way.

Two strong-minded, dedicated women who played a major role in the suffrage campaign were Carrie Chapman Catt (1859–1947) and Anna Howard Shaw (1847–1919). Mrs. Catt was one of the founders in 1890 of the National Woman Suffrage Association and became its president in 1900. Dr. Shaw (she earned degrees in both theology and medicine, but had difficulty in finding a denomination that would ordain her as a clergyman) was president of the association from 1904 to 1915.

Another noisy and controversial agitation was the temperance movement which was also gathering strength. Campaigns to secure prohibition, or at least to promote temperance, were not new in the United States. The Woman's Christian Temperance Union had been founded in 1874, and the Anti-Saloon League in 1893. The United States in its rougher frontier days had had a reputation for containing a large number of hard drinkers and the oppression of factory life at low wages was generally thought to have driven the new urban lower classes to drink. In any event, reformers, supported chiefly by the more conservative Protestant denominations, began to exert pressure on state and city officials to clamp controls on the sale of liquor, or to secure referendums in which a majority of the voters could deny the right to drink to everyone. As early as 1900 five states were "dry" at a time when in the large cities there was one saloon for every 200 inhabitants. By 1917, when national prohibition was adopted as a wartime measure to save grain, labor and production facilities, about two-thirds of the states were dry and in others there were local areas where alcoholic beverages had been voted illegal.

The most spectacular crusader for prohibition was Carry Nation (1846–1911). An awesome woman, six feet tall and weighing 180 pounds, whose first husband had died a drunkard, Mrs. Nation began her career as a saloon-smasher in 1900. The next year she began using a hatchet, and that became her symbol. Her technique was very simple: she went into a saloon with her hatchet and began laying about her to break bottles, glasses, mirrors and anything else within reach. She was arrested and fined many times but she never gave up her crusade.

Another movement, quieter and less successful than either that for women's votes or prohibition, was aimed at bringing about the end of war and a state of international peace in which disputes between nations would be resolved by peaceful means. This movement had behind it the efforts of some of America's leading citizens, such as Nicholas Murray Butler of Columbia University, David Starr Jordan of Stanford University, A. Lawrence Lowell of Harvard University, and the inventor, Thomas A. Edison. It also had the support of organizations with well-filled treasuries. Andrew Carnegie established the Carnegie Endowment for International Peace in 1910 with a gift of $10,000,000, while the next year a Boston publisher, Edwin Ginn, created the World Peace Foundation. Some high government officials thought war could be avoided if governments would agree to arbitrate their disputes. President Taft believed strongly in the judicial approach, but in 1911 the Senate refused to approve his arbitration treaties with Great Britain and France. A few years later, under President Wilson and Secretary of State Bryan, a number of such treaties were negotiated and approved, but, ironically, this was at the time World War I was about to burst forth.

In the peace movement the most unusual effort, and the most disastrous, was the Ford Peace Ship of 1915. Well-meaning but impractical idealists convinced Henry Ford, who was a genius at producing low-priced cars but still a naive country boy in other respects, that he ought to sponsor a "peace ship" which would go to Europe with a group of scholars, reformers, publicists, clergymen and others on board. The expedition sailed, with more than fifty reporters also aboard, most of whom found more to ridicule than to praise. Not surprisingly, the peace ship's passengers accomplished nothing in trying to get the leaders of nations locked in a life-and-death struggle to stop fighting in the name of Henry Ford.

Some of the major events of the progressive era were those over which man had no control. Listed generally under such headings as accidents or acts of God, they included earthquakes, ship-sinkings, fires and other assorted troubles that came to human beings.

For the United States the worst disaster was the San Francisco earthquake of April 18, 1906. Early that morning a tremor shook the city by the Golden Gate and knocked down many buildings. The quake's worst damage, however, came not from the first shock but from the fires that soon broke out and swept the city. Gas lines fed the fire while broken water mains deprived the fire department of most of the water supply it needed. For three days, firemen, soldiers and volunteers fought the spreading flames with water and dynamite. Finally the fire was brought under control but by that time 490 blocks had been ruined, 25,000 buildings were gone, 225,000 people were homeless and more than 450 persons had lost their lives. Among those who had been visiting the city at the time and who escaped injury were operatic tenor Enrico Caruso and actor John Barrymore. San Francisco's residents almost at once set about rebuilding their city. A bank, although itself burned out, offered to lend money to its depositors to help them get businesses going again, department stores began to buy new stocks, and the whole nation sent aid, both through the government in Washington and through many individual citizens.

At sea the most terrible disaster was the sinking of the British liner *Titanic*. The *Titanic*, heralded as the fastest, most luxurious ship in the world, and also unsinkable, sailed on its maiden voyage from England to the United States in April, 1912. The night of April 14–15, her fifth night out, she ran into an iceberg in the Atlantic south of Newfoundland. Whether the ship failed to heed iceberg warnings because she was too intent on setting a new speed record, or whether those in charge really believed she was unsinkable, is not certain. It soon became apparent that the splendid ship was going down. The tragedy was compounded by the discovery that there were not enough lifeboats for everyone, by the panicky behavior of some crewmen and passengers, and by the failure of rescue ships to arrive as soon as they might have.

Even so, there was heroism and gallantry. Men stood aside so that women and children might be saved. Many families were separated forever, but Mrs. Isidor Straus refused to leave her husband of many years and they went down together. Two hours after the crash, as the ship went beneath the waves, its band was still bravely playing on deck. The maiden voyage of the biggest passenger ship ever built had attracted the wealthy and the socially prominent, leaders in various fields, such as the John Jacob Astors, Francis D. Millett, the painter, and Archie Butts, President Taft's military aide. Many of them were among the approximately 1,500 persons who lost their lives out of a combined passenger and crew list of about 2,200 persons. There had been no ship disaster like this since the *General Slocum* caught fire and collapsed in New York's East River in June, 1904. It was carrying about 1,400 persons, mostly women and children, on a church-sponsored excursion, and 1,021 of them perished.

One of the most tragic fires of the era occurred in a theater, another in a factory. On December 30, 1903, fire swept the Iroquois Theater in Chicago, killing 602 persons, most of the patrons dying in the panic when they stampeded and blocked the exits. A fire that caused a horrified public to demand more stringent laws concerning working conditions occurred in Manhattan on March 26, 1911, in a sweatshop, the Triangle Waist Company. The 850 employees, most of them young women, were trapped by locked doors and inadequate exits. Of them, 145 perished.

In October, 1910, a dispute between union labor and anti-union forces in Los Angeles led to a bomb explosion which blew up the *Los Angeles Times* building and killed twenty people. The confession of one of those responsible was a heavy blow to the labor movement which had been trying to build up a reputation for responsibility. In 1900 and again in 1914 nature hit Galveston, Texas, with stunning force. The first disaster was caused by a hurricane and tidal wave which killed 6,000 persons. In the process of rebuilding, Galveston created the new city commission type of government to achieve businesslike action. Fourteen years later another tidal wave struck Galveston, but this time the death toll was held to 275.

Preparedness Day parades were held around the country in 1916, sponsored by those who thought the United States should increase its armed forces because of the growing danger that the country would be drawn into World War I. During such a parade in San Francisco on July 12, someone set off a bomb which killed ten people and wounded forty. Thomas J. Mooney, a labor leader who had been involved in several violent union struggles, was arrested, along with some others, and charged with the crime. Mooney was convicted and sentenced to death. His conviction was followed by agitation here and abroad to free him because many people believed in his innocence and there was no doubt that perjured testimony had been given at his trial. His sentence was commuted to life imprisonment in 1918, but many organizations kept up a "free Tom Mooney" campaign until finally, in 1939, the governor of California pardoned him.

Two other disasters were directly related to the war. The Black Tom explosion, so named for the part of Jersey City, New Jersey, in which it occurred, killed two persons and caused $22,000,000 worth of damage. It was set off by German saboteurs in July, 1916, even though the United States was not yet in the war, to demolish a store of munitions. The next year in the harbor of Halifax, Nova Scotia, a vessel carrying explosives was accidentally rammed by another ship. The explosion that followed killed about 1,800 people, injured 20,000 and destroyed a large part of the city.

The most talked about murder of the era was that in which Stanford White, the prominent architect, then fifty-three, was shot and killed by Harry K. Thaw, a rich playboy. On the evening of June 25, 1906, White appeared at the roof-garden theater of Madison Square Garden. (He had designed the Garden and lived in the tower.) While he was seated at a table, Thaw walked up to him and shot him fatally with a pistol. Thaw claimed he had done the deed to protect his wife, a former chorus girl and model named Evelyn Nesbit, from White's attentions. Thaw's trial became a sensational drama that fascinated the whole country. At his first trial the jury could not reach a verdict. At the second, in 1908, he was declared "not guilty because insane" and committed to a state hospital for the criminally insane. During a long series of legal maneuvers by his lawyers, Thaw in 1913 escaped from the hospital. He was found in Canada and brought back. In 1915 another trial declared him sane and he was released.

A murder case with ugly implications of prejudice and class feeling began in Atlanta, Georgia, in April, 1913, when a fourteen-year-old girl, Mary Phagan, was found murdered in a pencil factory. The manager of the factory, Leo Frank, was Jewish and had come from New York. He was accused of the murder and convicted, although the evidence against him was flimsy. The governor of the state commuted Frank's death sentence to life-imprisonment, just before he was scheduled for execution in June, 1915. This further enraged lower-class groups eager to find a specific object for their anger against northern capitalists who, they believed, exploited poor southerners, especially women. A mob raided the penitentiary, carried Frank across most of the state and lynched him.

All the actions of men and the events of nature had to take a back seat to Halley's Comet. It was named for Edmund Halley who observed it in 1682, although there are records to trace it back to 240 B.C. It had last been seen in 1758 and was now expected to pass near the earth in 1910. As the time came near, some would-be seers predicted the end of the earth. Enough people were frightened so that comet pills, which were supposed to protect the taker from the comet's dire effects, were a salable item in New York. In Pennsylvania many miners refused to go to work the day the comet was due on the grounds that they didn't want to spend the last day of their lives underground. In Milwaukee two men were said to have committed suicide, while in Iowa a farmer hid his family and his livestock in a cave. On May 18, the earth passed through the fiery tail of Halley's Comet while thousands sought vantage points from which to see the spectacle. The earth survived, as it was to survive more dangerous events in the near future.

14 *Woodrow Wilson and War*

PRESIDENT WILSON would have preferred to stand for reelection in 1916 on his record as a progressive reformer, but the war in Europe now overshadowed all else. The Democrats, who by this time had most of the progressive-minded voters in their camp, were happy to renominate Wilson, but the Republicans had to find a new candidate. Ex-President Roosevelt left little doubt but that he was willing to do battle once again, but the party machinery was controlled by those who were more conservative and who had not forgiven Roosevelt's defection in 1912 to run on the Progressive Party ticket. The ruling Republicans, seeking to present a candidate who was conservative at heart but who had some aura of reform about him, chose Charles Evans Hughes (1862–1948) as their candidate.

Hughes had first become prominent in 1905–06 when he headed the investigation into the shady dealings of the life insurance companies. This defense of the public interest won Hughes the Republican nomination and election twice as governor of New York State, where he ably managed a reform and progressive administration. In 1910 President Taft appointed him an associate justice of the Supreme Court and he held that post until he resigned in 1916 to run for the presidency. Hughes was a handsome, impressive man with a magnificent beard, but he was stiff and formal in his public appearances.

In the campaign, the Democrats made the most of the slogan,

"He kept us out of war," although Wilson never promised that he could continue to do so indefinitely. Hughes might have won had he not unintentionally snubbed Governor Hiram Johnson of California when he visited that state. As it was, the election was very close and it was more than twenty-four hours after the last polls closed before it became clear that Wilson had carried California by fewer than 4,000 votes and with it the election by 277 to 254 votes in the Electoral College. Wilson received about 9,130,000 popular votes to Hughes's 8,530,000.

Wilson's—and the nation's—demanding problem was what to do about the war that had been tearing Europe apart since the summer of 1914. On June 28, 1914, a young Serb, Gavrilo Princip, shot and killed the Austro-Hungarian Archduke Francis Ferdinand and his wife. The Austrian government used the assassination as an excuse to crush the small Serbian nation, and a month after the killing declared war. Russia, as protector of her fellow Slavs, ordered general mobilization. Germany, in turn, used this as an excuse to deliver an ultimatum to Russia on behalf of her ally, Austria-Hungary. The Germans declared war on Russia, which brought France into the conflict on the side of her ally, the Russian czar. By August 4, Great Britain was also in the fight, having declared war on Germany because of the invasion of neutral Belgium. Within less than a month, Japan, on the far side of the world, joined in on the side of Russia, France and Great Britain.

War on such a worldwide scale shocked people all over the world. Many believed that such a thing just couldn't happen in the twentieth century. When the armies did march against each other, the general reaction in the United States was that it was none of our concern. The country had a long tradition of neutrality, and of staying out of Europe's quarrels, which were somehow supposed to be less honorable and more selfish than fights we might get into. President

Wilson, then not much more than a year into his first term, addressed his countrymen, in part:

> The United States must be neutral in fact as well as in name during these days that are to try men's souls. We must be impartial in thought as well as in action, must put a curb upon our sentiments as well as upon every transaction that might be construed as a preference of one party to the struggle before another.

In practice most Americans were not neutral in their feelings even if they wanted to stay out of the war. Irish-Americans had good reasons for wishing ill to the British, and German-Americans had natural ties with their, or their fathers', homeland. Beyond that all the ties of history and language drew America to the British, while France's help in the American Revolution was still remembered.

For the first few months it looked as though the war would not last long and that Germany would be an easy victor. The Kaiser's armies swept through Belgium and France and almost reached Paris before they were brought to a halt. On the eastern front Germany achieved equally spectacular victories over the ill-prepared and poorly equipped Russian forces, but here, too, the advance ground to a halt. There was a stalemate on both fronts which turned into bloody trench-warfare for four long years. Turkey and Bulgaria entered the war on the side of the Central Powers, but Italy, which had been a member of the Triple Alliance of Germany and Austria-Hungary, came in on the side of the Allies. In 1915 the Allies staged the Gallipoli campaign to force passage of the Dardanelles in Asia Minor, but Winston Churchill's plan met disastrous defeat. That same year the Germans first used poison gas but the brief advantage it gained them was not decisive. The next year the British introduced the tank in warfare but they, too, failed to exploit the new weapon enough to break the deadlock. It was in 1916, also, that the bloodiest struggle of all began at Verdun in France where the Germans and French suffered immense casualties, with the latter holding onto the ground with incredible stubbornness.

The German battle fleet was kept in its home ports and the German colonies in Africa and Asia were seized by the British, French and Japanese. Individual German warships caused considerable damage as commerce raiders, but this had more nuisance value than anything else. The German fleet in May, 1916, ventured forth to give battle to the British fleet at Jutland. The British suffered heavier losses than the Germans, but the Germans retired and never came out again.

Meanwhile, even though the United States was not a belligerent, the war was having an increasing effect on the nation, especially on its economy. The outbreak of war aggravated a trend toward depression that the American economy was showing at the time. The New York Stock Exchange closed down for a while. The price of wheat and cotton dropped. Then, as the nations of Europe began reorganizing their economies on a wartime basis, business in the United States improved. Since the Allied powers controlled the seas, most of the wartime trade was with them. Germany had no practical way of transporting American goods to its shores through the British blockade. American trade with the Allied nations increased from $825,000,000 in 1914 to $3,214,000,000 in 1916, by which time about 40 per cent of it was accounted for by munitions.

At the start Great Britain and France were able to pay cash, but soon the unprecedented expenses of waging a modern war made them seek credit. The American government's attitude at first was that it was improper to lend money to any belligerent. This was soon modified to allow short-term bank credits. By September, 1915, it was clear that unless the Allies were allowed to float long-term loans here, they could not carry on the war and the United States economy might collapse. The ban on loans was dropped and J. P. Morgan and Company, which had been agent for the Allies for some time, floated a half-billion-dollar loan for England and France. By the time the United States entered the war in 1917, the total borrowed had reached $2,000,000,000.

While the fighting was going on in Europe, and while American trade and industry were being altered by events, there was another struggle on the diplomatic front to defend what the Wilson administration considered the rights of the United States as a formal neutral. Under the old rules of warfare, merchantmen were not armed, and ships that attacked them were supposed to give warning and to see to the safety of the passengers and the crew. In World War I, however, because of the life-and-death nature of the war, and because of new weapons, both sides abandoned the old rules. The British announced a long list of contraband articles and seized ships carrying them to the Central Powers. In early 1915 the Germans declared that a war zone existed around the British Isles and the coast of France, and that they would sink all ships venturing into the zone. The British began to arm their merchantmen. What brought about the greatest change in war at sea, however, was the submarine. The German command felt that its only chance to defeat England was to cut off her vital seaborne commerce. Since the German fleet was inferior, her only hope lay with her U-boats, which she began to build in increasing numbers. A submarine on the surface was a very fragile target, and a cramped underseas boat had little room for additional persons. Consequently, the U-boat's tactic was to find an enemy ship and sink it with torpedoes without warning.

While the United States protested against the Allied blockade and against the seizure of merchandise, this aspect of the struggle was never too serious because no American lives were lost and indemnity could always be claimed for the seized goods. The German tactics, however, endangered lives, and it was not long before one such event brought the United States to the brink of war. On May 7, 1915, the British liner *Lusitania,* unarmed but carrying some munitions, was torpedoed by a German U-boat off the Irish coast. She sank with a loss of 1,198 lives, of which 128 were Americans. The country was horrified by this kind of warfare and Wilson protested vigorously to the German government—so vigorously in fact that William Jennings Bryan, who believed in peace at almost any price, resigned as secretary of state. He was succeeded by Robert Lansing who was very much pro-Ally.

Germany, fearing that the United States would enter the war on the Allied side, said she would spare all large passenger ships, but two months later a U-boat torpedoed the *Arabic* with the loss of two American lives. Now Germany promised not to sink passenger ships without warning, but in February, 1916, Germany warned that her U-boats would sink any armed merchantmen they came upon. After a strong American protest over an incident a month later, the Germans drew back somewhat and said they would also warn merchant ships before sinking them. The Germans asked that in return for this pledge, the United States get the Allies to give up their blockade of Germany. Wilson ignored this part of the deal the Kaiser was trying to make, but he could not have done anything about it anyway. However, he had now taken such a strong line, and had continued to defend so strenuously the "right" of neutral Americans to go anywhere on any ship, that one more incident would almost certainly bring the country into the conflict.

During this same period there was an internal debate between those who thought the United States should build up its defenses in case it became involved in the war, and those who felt that doing anything of this kind would increase the chances of involvement. Ex-President Roosevelt had been an early, and as usual a vociferous, advocate of preparedness. Popular opinion and the Wilson administration were opposed until the sinking of the *Lusitania.* This event aroused many people and it was shortly afterwards that Wilson asked the War and Navy departments to make recommendations for strengthening the nation's defense establishment. In November, 1915, the President made formal proposals to the country. In mid-1916 Congress, after much wrangling, approved one bill to more than double the strength of the regular Army and to greatly increase the National Guard, and another bill which authorized the construction of a large number of warships of different sizes. These acts were followed by a bill to build up the merchant marine. Finally, a new tax law, needed to help pay for preparedness, increased the income tax and put considerably more of the burden of it on the wealthy than heretofore.

Early in 1917, after Wilson had been reelected but before he had been inaugurated for his second term, events pushed the nation ever nearer war. Wilson had asked the warring powers in December, 1916, to state their war aims to him and they did. Both sides, in effect, asked for terms that would have meant an admission of complete defeat by the other. On January 22, Wilson made one of his most notable speeches in which he offered America's cooperation in establishing a lasting peace if all parties would agree to a "peace without victory." Nothing came of this and on January 31 the German government announced that its U-boats would immediately resume unrestricted warfare, sinking any and all ships in the war zones. Wilson felt he had no choice except to break off diplomatic relations with Germany, which he did on February 3.

The next blow to a nation that was becoming more and more reconciled to the likelihood of war fell on March 1 when the President revealed to the public the contents of the "Zimmerman telegram," so named for the German foreign secretary. The message in question had been sent by him to the German minister in Mexico City in January, and the British intelligence service had decoded it. The note told the German minister in Mexico that, in the event the United States went to war against Germany, he should propose to the Mexican government that it join in war against America. Mexico would be rewarded with the return of the "lost territory" that now made up the states of Texas, New Mexico and Arizona. Further, the German minister was to try to get the Mexicans to talk the Japanese into switching sides and to go to war against the United States. The nation was outraged at Germany as it had never been before.

In the meantime Wilson had been trying to get Congress to give him authority to arm American merchant ships, but a filibuster led by Senator LaFollette defeated the bill. Wilson ordered the arming on his own, after Congress adjourned on March 4. Germany's new submarine-warfare policy resulted in the sinking of an unarmed American merchantman on March 12 and six days later U-boats torpedoed three more ships.

In Europe the casualty list was now in the millions, and still the slaughter went on. While neither side could claim victory was near, the Allies did seem to be getting the worst of it. On March 15 the Russian monarchy toppled when Czar Nicholas II was forced to abdicate. This weakened the Allies' strength, but on the other hand people pointed out that there was no longer any despotic monarchy on the Allied side to embarrass democratic America.

Wilson, who had tried to keep the country out of war, finally, after agonizing soul-searching, went before Congress on the evening of April 2 to ask for a declaration of war against Germany. At the close of his speech he said:

> It is a distressing and oppressive duty, Gentlemen of the Congress, which I have performed in thus addressing you. There are, it may be, many months of fiery trial and sacrifice ahead of us. It is a fearful thing to lead this great peaceful people into war, into the most terrible and disastrous of all wars, civilization itself seeming to be in the balance. But the right is more precious than peace, and we shall fight for the things which we have always carried nearest our hearts—for democracy, for the right of those who submit to authority to have a voice in their own governments, for the rights and liberties of small nations, for a universal dominion of right by such a concert of

> free peoples as shall bring peace and safety to all nations and make the world itself at last free.
>
> To such a task we dedicate our lives and our fortunes, everything that we are and everything that we have, with the pride of those who know that the day has come when America is privileged to spend her blood and her might for the principles that gave her birth and the peace which she has treasured. God helping her, she can do no other.

Wilson received a tremendous ovation from almost all members of Congress of both parties, but back in the White House he said sadly to an aide:
"Think of what it was they were applauding. My message today was a message of death for our young men. How strange it seems to applaud that."

Opinion both in and out of Congress favored war. On April 4, the Senate approved the declaration by a vote of 82 to 6; two days later the House gave its approval, 373 to 50.

The most devastating war in history had been going on for nearly three years before the United States, the newest and youngest world power, the dominating nation of the Western Hemisphere, was drawn in, or joined in. Should the nation have entered the war earlier? Should it—or could it—have stayed out altogether? To answer such questions it is necessary to examine Wilson's motives and policies. At first Wilson certainly wanted to stay out. The idea of such a war appalled him. Yet he was a moralist; he saw international relations in moral terms and so certain actions were "right" and some were "wrong." He was also at heart a nineteenth-century idealist who believed in the idea of progress. It was easy to extend to the world stage the attitudes of the progressive reformers in the cities of America. Wilson looked forward to a peaceful international order based on democratic world opinion. To this was added the idea, not new with Wilson, that the United States was somehow better, morally, than other countries, and had a mission to save humanity. Wilson would have been happiest if he could have persuaded the warring nations to let him and his country mediate the conflict and set up a new world system.

In the course of the war years, however, Wilson's policies and actions were not impartial and entirely above the conflict. Consciously or not, he favored the Allies. He said he was standing by old established rules of international law, but his actions benefited the British who controlled the seas. He refused to face the fact that the submarine had changed warfare in such a way as to make old rules and customs impossible of acceptance by the side that depended on the submarine—in this case, Germany. The two sides were not treated equally. At the same time, America's economic interests came more and more to call for an Allied victory and a German defeat. Less tangible but of some importance was the feeling that a German victory, because imperial Germany seemed undemocratic and militaristic, would be a long-term threat to the United States. For many years the United States had relied chiefly on the British fleet to protect the Atlantic Ocean for the English-speaking peoples.

No less important was the image of the two sides that grew and took ever-larger shape in the minds of the American people. British propaganda was efficient and successful; German propaganda was heavy-handed and annoying. Germany invaded poor, little, neutral Belgium without provocation, which was true even if the atrocity stories perpetrated by the British as to how cruelly the Germans treated the conquered Belgians weren't. The choice came to be almost as simple as in a western movie in which the "bad guys" fight the "good guys."

So it was that most Americans, when the die was cast, went to war as to a crusade. They fought in the spirit of their president's war message. Whether rightly or wrongly, they set out to accomplish for the world the goal Herbert Croly in 1909 in *The Promise of American Life* had set for the nation:

> What a democratic nation must do is not to accept human nature as it is, but to move in the direction of its improvement.

America's entry into the war meant the end of the progressive era and the kind of domestic reforms the progressives had set out to achieve and which they had partly secured. It was to be a few years before a disappointed nation found that world peace was even more difficult an accomplishment than honesty in city government.

Reading List

In the following list the publisher and the date of publication are those of the original edition. If that edition is paperbound, it is so indicated. A number of the other titles are available in paperbound editions as well as in the edition listed below.

AARON, DANIEL. *Men of Good Hope: A Story of American Progressives.* New York: Oxford University Press, Inc., 1951.

ALLEN, FREDERICK LEWIS. *The Big Change: America Transforms Itself, 1900–1950.* New York: Harper & Bros., 1952.

———. *The Lords of Creation.* New York: Harper & Bros., 1935.

BEALE, HOWARD K. *Theodore Roosevelt and the Rise of America to World Power.* Baltimore: The Johns Hopkins Press, 1956.

BLUM, JOHN MORTON. *The Republican Roosevelt.* Cambridge: Harvard University Press, 1954.

———. *Woodrow Wilson and the Politics of Morality.* Boston: Little, Brown & Co., 1956.

BOARDMAN, FON W., JR. *America and the Jazz Age: A History of the 1920's.* New York: Henry Z. Walck, Inc., 1968.

BURCHARD, JOHN, and BUSH-BROWN, ALBERT. *The Architecture of America: A Social and Cultural History.* Abridged ed. Boston: Little, Brown & Co., 1966.

CHURCHILL, ALLEN. *Remember When.* New York: Golden Press, Inc., 1967.

COCHRAN, THOMAS C. *The American Business System: A Historical Perspective, 1900–1955.* Cambridge: Harvard University Press, 1957.

CUNLIFFE, MARCUS. *The Literature of the United States.* Baltimore: Penguin Books, 1961. Paper.

DULLES, FOSTER RHEA. *America's Rise to World Power, 1898–1954.* New York: Harper & Bros., 1954.

FAULKNER, HAROLD U. *American Economic History.* 8th ed. New York: Harper & Row, Publishers, 1960.

GARRATY, JOHN A. *Woodrow Wilson.* New York: Alfred A. Knopf, Inc., 1956.

GINGER, RAY. *Age of Excess: The United States from 1877 to 1914.* New York: The Macmillan Co., 1965.

GLAAB, CHARLES N., and BROWN, A. THEODORE. *A History of Urban America.* New York: The Macmillan Co., 1967.

GOLDMAN, ERIC F. *Rendezvous with Destiny: A History of Modern American Reform.* Revised ed., Abridged by the author. New York: Alfred A. Knopf, Inc., 1956. Paper.

GREEN, CONSTANCE MCLAUGHLIN. *The Rise of Urban America.* New York: Harper & Row, Publishers, 1965.

HANDLIN, OSCAR. *Immigration as a Factor in American History.* Englewood Cliffs: Prentice-Hall, Inc., 1959. Paper.

———. *The Uprooted: The Epic Story of the Great Migrations that Made the American People.* Boston: Little, Brown & Co., 1951.

HANSEN, MARCUS LEE. *The Immigrant in American History.* Cambridge: Harvard University Press, 1940.

HAYS, SAMUEL P. *The Response to Industrialism: 1885–1914.* Chicago: University of Chicago Press, 1957.

HIGHAM, JOHN. *Strangers in the Land: Patterns of American Nativism, 1860–1925.* 2nd ed. New Brunswick: Rutgers University Press, 1963.

HOFSTADTER, RICHARD. *The Age of Reform: from Bryan to F.D.R.* New York: Alfred A. Knopf, Inc., 1955.

——— (ed.). *The Progressive Movement, 1900–1915.* Englewood Cliffs: Prentice-Hall, Inc., 1963. Paper.

HUNTER, SAM. *Modern American Painting and Sculpture.* New York: Dell Publishing Co., Inc., 1959. Paper.

JONES, MALDWYN ALLEN. *American Immigration.* Chicago: University of Chicago Press, 1960.

KAZIN, ALFRED. *On Native Grounds: An Interpretation of Modern American Prose Literature.* New York: Harcourt, Brace & Co., 1942.

LINK, ARTHUR S. *Woodrow Wilson and the Progressive Era, 1910–1917.* New York: Harper & Bros., 1954.

LORD, WALTER. *The Good Years: From 1900 to the First World War.* New York: Harper & Row, Publishers, 1960.

LYNES, RUSSELL. *The Tastemakers.* New York: Harper & Bros., 1949.

MARSHALL, S. L. A. *The American Heritage History of World War I.* New York: American Heritage Publishing Co., Inc., 1964.

MAY, HENRY F. *The End of American Innocence: A Study of the First Years of Our Own Time, 1912–1917.* New York: Alfred A. Knopf, Inc., 1959.

MILLIS, WALTER. *The Martial Spirit: A Study of Our War with Spain.* Boston: Houghton Mifflin Co., 1931.

MORRIS, LLOYD. *Postscript to Yesterday: American Life and Thought, 1896–1946.* New York: Random House, Inc., 1947.

MOWRY, GEORGE E. *Theodore Roosevelt and the Progressive Movement.* Madison: University of Wisconsin Press, 1946.

———. *The Era of Theodore Roosevelt and the Birth of Modern America, 1900–1912.* New York: Harper & Bros., 1958.

PRINGLE, HENRY F. *Theodore Roosevelt: A Biography.* Revised and abridged. New York: Harcourt, Brace & World, Inc., 1956. Paper.

RAE, JOHN B. *The American Automobile: A Brief History.* Chicago: University of Chicago Press, 1965.

SINCLAIR, ANDREW. *The Better Half: The Emancipation of the American Woman.* New York: Harper & Row, Publishers, 1965.

STEFFENS, LINCOLN. *The Shame of the Cities.* New York: McClure, Philips & Co., 1904.

STOVER, JOHN F. *American Railroads.* Chicago: University of Chicago Press, 1961.

SULLIVAN, MARK. *Our Times: The United States, 1900–1925.* Vol. III: *Pre-War America.* New York: Charles Scribner's Sons, 1930.

SWANBERG, W. A. *Dreiser.* New York: Charles Scribner's Sons, 1965.

TAYLOR, DEEMS. *A Pictorial History of the Movies.* New York: Simon & Schuster, Inc., 1943.

WALETT, FRANCIS G. *Economic History of the United States.* 2nd ed. New York: Barnes & Noble, Inc., 1963. Paper.

WECTER, DIXON. *The Hero in America: A Chronicle of Hero-Worship.* New York: Charles Scribner's Sons, 1941.

WHITE, MORTON. *Social Thought in America: The Revolt Against Formalism.* New York: The Viking Press, 1949.

WIEBE, ROBERT H. *The Search for Order, 1877–1920.* New York: Hill and Wang, 1967.

Index